What Mothers Everywhere
Are Saying about Sandra Swenson

Finally, someone understands what it is to be the mother of an addict! I have been looking for a resource, a sense of hope, and found it. — DEBI

•

Sandy Swenson has helped me understand the difference between loving my son and enabling the addict. — MARSHA

•

Sandy puts into elegant and yet simple words EXACTLY what it is to be a mother of an addict. I'm crying knowing that I'm not alone in feeling all of this. — MAGGIE

•

Sandy continues to astound me with her gifts. She has changed the lives of so many of us with her astounding experience, strength, and hope. — ASHLEY

•

If you haven't read Sandy Swenson yet, you must! Everything she writes will leave you saying, "YESSSSSS! I did that! I felt that!" — DONNA

•

Sandy made me realize this story has not ended yet! This is not a perfectly wrapped up little packa~~~ ~~
put aside now. Sandy's
a way to deal with too
it differently. Thank y
Unfortunately, I can rel

T0017951

• HAZELDEN MEDITATIONS •

Tending Dandelions

Honest Meditations
for Mothers with Addicted Children

SANDRA SWENSON

Hazelden Publishing
Center City, Minnesota 55012
hazelden.org/bookstore

Library of Congress Cataloging-in-Publication Data

Names: Swenson, Sandra, 1959- author.
Title: Tending dandelions : honest meditations for mothers with addicted
    children / Sandra Swenson.
Description: Center City, Minnesota : Hazelden Publishing, 2017. |
Identifiers: LCCN 2017017710 (print) | LCCN 2017033228 (ebook) |
    ISBN 9781616497217 (epub) | ISBN 9781616497200 (pbk.)
Subjects: LCSH: Parents of drug addicts. | Parents of alcoholics. | Meditations.
Classification: LCC HV5805 (ebook) | LCC HV5805 .S94 2017 (print) |
    DDC 362.29/13--dc23
LC record available at https://lccn.loc.gov/2017017710

Editor's notes

This publication is intended to support personal growth and should not be thought
of as a substitute for the advice of health care professionals. The author's advice
and viewpoints are her own.

Quotations at the end of meditations that do not have an attribution are from
Sandra Swenson. The quotations at the end of pages 15, 16, 19, 20, 36, 38, 47,
51, 53, 91, 111, 124, 142, 165, and 204 are adapted from Sandra Swenson's book
The Joey Song (2014, Central Recovery Press).

The art on page vii comes from iStock.com/TinaAmber. The art on the part
divider pages comes from iStock.com/aqua_marinka.

25 24 23 22 21   3 4 5 6

COVER AND INTERIOR DESIGN: TERRI KINNE
TYPESETTING: TRINA CHRISTENSEN
DEVELOPMENT EDITOR: VANESSA TORRADO
PRODUCTION EDITOR: HEATHER SILSBEE

Together We Are Stronger

This book is dedicated to the parents living
in the place where love and addiction meet—
a place where help enables and hope hurts.

For parents trying to figure out the difference
between helping their child live and
helping their child die.

For parents grieving the loss of a child
who is still alive. For parents needing to
find a recovery of their own.

You are not alone.

Hugs and hope,
Sandy

dandelion | *noun* | dan•de•li•on \ˈdan-də-ˌlī-ən\

[from Anglo-French *dent de lion*, literally, lion's tooth]

: vibrant golden-yellow flower. underappreciated. thrives in harsh conditions. shabby tufts scatter the flowers of tomorrow.

: a weed or a wish, depending on point of view.

: strong. like a *roar*.

In This Book

From One Mother to Another

We may often feel fragile, but we are strong.

And we are many.

As mothers of children suffering with addiction, we do battle with a disease that oozes misunderstanding and shame. Alone and afraid, we try to do the right thing— even when we're not sure what that right thing *is*. We try to hold our families and ourselves together, even when it feels like we're falling apart. We feel every pain our child feels, no matter the distance (in miles or years). We try to carry on, even when our heart is breaking in two. But, as tired and tattered as we may be, like the deceptively delicate dandelion, we moms are made to persevere.

Together, we're traveling a most unwanted, unanticipated, and unclear journey—for a lifetime. Whatever happens next may or may not follow a neat or hopeful path. So, we all need to find our own inner dandelion; we all need to take a close look at the things we don't want to look at—the things lurking around in this place where love and addiction meet—so we're as strong as we can be. My wish is that the "ponderments" contained within this book—the thoughts laid bare for you to think about—will help you achieve that.

Whenever I sit down to write, I write as a mom, as the mom of an addict, and, specifically, as the mom of a son—a son who has not yet found his own recovery. I write as a mom who has begun her own recovery, though her son has not. My writing comes from deep within this particular mix. However, while the voice burbling up comes from the well of my own experience, it is intended to be a reflection of the heart and soul of every mother of an addict. It is intended to help put words to your own thoughts and feelings. To help you heal.

Recovery is a process we all share. It's not only for the health and well-being of our beloved addicts, but for our families—and ourselves—too. On the road to recovery, we pass through several stages—sometimes again and again (and all cattywompus), and in our own good time. The ponderments on these pages, collected as a set of meditations, reflect those stages.

When addiction first takes root in our child, we may be completely unaware, but once we've heaved ourselves over the monstrous hurdle of realization, the recovery journey begins. We learn, we grow. We cry, we wilt. We learn the value of nurturing ourselves. We find strength, we bloom. And finally, like fields of frazzled flowers, we scatter seeds of truth and goodness, changing the dynamic of this place where love and addiction meet. One by one, and one after another, we are carried aloft by the *hope,* the *help,* and the *beating hearts* of other mothers who love a child suffering with addiction.

We may often feel fragile, but we are strong.

And we are many.

We have the power to overpower the destruction that addiction spreads.

PART ONE
Take Root

Where Love and Addiction Meet

The first time my child reached his dimpled little hand out for mine, I was there. And I've tried to be there every time he's reached out to me—and even when he hasn't— ever since. Until, that is, my child became an addict. Addiction has made such a mess of things that I'm no longer sure if I should be within range when he reaches out (or even when he doesn't).

I don't know if my help is hurting this child of mine. I don't know if I should stay silent or speak up. I'm not sure how to love without doing the things that seem loving, or where to put the dreams and conversations and hugs that have gone unused and are piling up. I don't know how to fill my empty arms, or where to put my love for this child who says he hates me. My heart doesn't understand this place where love and addiction meet—it's all confused about what it means to be my son's mom.

I cannot be there for my child in the way life intended, but *my love* will always be there whenever he reaches out—and even when he doesn't.

I mean, it is the most impossible love . . . it's absolutely fine for me to teach you how to walk and talk, and then you grow up and you head off in the wrong direction toward a cliff. And I'm supposed to just stand there and wave.

— *BECAUSE I SAID SO*

Before My Child Was an Addict

Before my son was an addict, he was a child. *My* child. But he could have been anyone's child. Before my son was an addict, he liked to joke around, give big hugs, and work hard and play harder. Sometimes, he also lied, or said things that were mean, sulked, or was crabby. In other words, my child was perfectly normal.

Even though he has done some bad things while being an addict, my son is not a *bad* person. He's a *sick* person. When addiction scooped up my child, it did so indiscriminately; my son, at his core, is one of the least "bad" people I know. Before my son was an addict, I used to judge the dusty addict on the corner very harshly. Now I know that being an addict isn't something anyone would choose.

I wish I hadn't waited for the worst to happen before I opened my eyes and heart. Before I looked beyond the addict's dust to the person he was meant to be. To the person my child could easily become . . . and did.

Addiction can happen to anyone.

Don't judge, just love. — ANONYMOUS

To Love an Addict

When I held my baby in my arms for the very first time, I rubbed my cheek on his fuzzy head and whispered, "I will love and protect you for as long as I live." I didn't know then that my baby would become an addict before becoming an adult, or that the addict taking his place would shred the meaning of those words to smithereens.

Slowly, at first, came the arrests and overdoses and big fat lies. My sweet child was turning into a stranger, manipulating me, using me, and twisting my love into knots. I was befuddled by this scary new world that I didn't even know I was in and that I knew nothing about. I thought I was just a regular mom stumbling through regular parenthood, but then I had to figure out how to be the mom of an addict. I had to figure out how to love my child without helping to hurt him, how to grieve the loss of my child—who's still alive—without dying, and how to trade shame and blame for strength.

To be the parent of an addict is to be an ambassador of truth and understanding. No more shame. No more silence.

To love an addict is to run out of tears.

I'm Not Ashamed

My child dreamed of becoming a firefighter, a fisherman, and a marine biologist when he grew up. Becoming an addict was not on his list. I know the child who dreamed those dreams and *he is a child to be proud of.* Tender and thoughtful and smart, he should be living his dreams. But my child isn't here—an addict has taken his place. Someone who looks like my child is hooked to the strings of an evil puppeteer and living a tortured life. Instead of fighting fires, my child is fighting demons. Instead of tying flies, he's flying high. Instead of reaching for the stars, he's reaching for a bottle. A life full of promise lost to a jug full of lies. Addiction took my child's dreams, chewed them up, and spat out a nightmare.

No, my child didn't dream of becoming an addict, and it certainly wasn't what I dreamed for him either. But I'm not ashamed my child is an addict. I'm sad he's an addict. By shining the light on addiction, I might just get him back.

*

Shame is a soul-eating emotion. — CARL JUNG

I Did Not Cause It

I did not cause my child to become an addict. As a parent, I don't possess that power.

When my children were little, I imagined I had all kinds of power. I could decide when it was time for their nap—but they might play in their cribs instead of sleeping. I could serve up a healthy dinner—but if they didn't want to eat the small mound of lima beans on their plates, *They Did Not!* I could teach my children right from wrong and good from bad, but my word alone often wasn't enough, and they experimented to see how those rights and wrongs worked. It soon became clear that while I could be their guide, my children were going to be who they were meant to be. My real power as a mother was simply to love them. (And to annoy them and make them mad.) As a parent, I was perceived to be too nosey, too clingy, and, on occasion, not clingy enough. I hurt my children's feelings. I made them feel angry, sad, unheard, and misunderstood. At times I hovered like a helicopter mom—at other moments I might have flown too far away.

I am an imperfect mom. But imperfect parenting does not cause children to become addicts.

If that were so, every child would grow up to be an addict.

✳

Too many people are spoiling their existence carrying needless guilt and shame. — ANONYMOUS

Dalliance Becomes Disease

Millions of people use millions of substances for millions of reasons—as an amusing little diversion, or on doctor's orders, or for drowning out difficult lives—yet they don't all become addicts. And, of those who do, not one of them chooses to live their life all snaggled up in addiction's noose. People may choose to use, but something else does the choosing at the point where substance abuse becomes addiction. Addiction happens when a renegade sip or snort or sniff crosses an invisible line between *want* and *need*.

I don't know why my child started using drugs and alcohol in his teens. And I don't know why addiction snuck up on him—picked him out of the substance-using crowd—and choked him. But I do know that *why he started* and *why he can't stop* are two different things.

Everything that comes before is changed forevermore, once dalliance—or doctor's orders—becomes disease.

In all my years as a physician, I have never, ever met an addicted person who wanted to be an addict.

— DR. NORA VOLKOW

Intoxicating Enticements: Myth One

He was just a kid when he made the choices that turned out to be bad choices. Choices that seemed like a good idea at the time. Cool choices, fun choices. He was just a kid when he was lured in by the intoxicating enticements that ruined his life.

Magazines and music and movies (and movie stars, musicians, and malls) radiate untarnished promises with glib little jokes or sly winks and nods. The fantastic illusion of substance abuse—the myth and the magic—is *alive and well* (although many of those who believed in the illusion, the myth, and the magic are not). The hard truths of the hard times, hard knocks, hard floors, and hard lives are kept under cover. The grit and the grime. The scratching, screaming, and scuttling about. The loss of family, friends, and the self. These things are hidden.

But he was just a kid when he made the choices that turned out to be bad choices. What seemed like a fun idea at the time turned into a crazed compulsion that's really no fun at all.

He'd opened Pandora's box, and there was no way to put its troubles back inside again. Even if she sat on the lid.

— KITTY FRENCH

Intoxicating Enticements: Myth Two

Lies, lies, and more lies. The alluring promises of substance abuse are all lies. No worries, no problems, and no consequences? *Lies.* The only truth in the lies is the *sneakiness* of addiction's influence on our culture in keeping drug and alcohol abuse alive.

The magazines and music and movies (and movie stars, musicians, and models) radiate untarnished promises of quick and easy addiction recovery. The fantastic illusion—in, out, and done—of relaxing for a month at a spa-like treatment center near the beach and coming out all fluffed and buffed (and buff) and cured is a lie. The hard truths of the hard work involved in addiction recovery are lost in the sparkle of the mirage. The detoxing and deep digging required to stay sober forever is hard, Hard, HARD. There is nothing quick or Zen about it.

The truth is that while recovery is absolutely achievable, *addiction is forever.* Addiction persists whether a person is in active recovery or not—so the hard work must go on as well. The promises, the intoxicating enticements, all of them, are a pretty package of lies.

It does not involve being "sent away" to rehab or residential where a miracle cure will be performed. Recovery from addiction is hard work. It is a lifelong pursuit that often entails failure, sometimes lots of failures.

— MICHAEL SCHOENHOFER

A Disease, Not a Disgrace

Misrepresented, misjudged, and mishandled. Addiction is a misunderstood tragedy, too often hushed up. Well, no more secrets. Not anymore.

My child is dying a slow death from the disease of addiction, enticed as a young teen to drink and do drugs by the very same culture that now looks with shock upon his addiction as a moral failure or reckless choice. Shame and blame and disdain.

So, for his sake, for my sake, for the sake of my family, I'm stepping out from the shadows.

When addiction is understood as a disease, it will be treated like a disease—but this is an understanding that will happen only when those of us who love an addict stop hiding addiction as though it's a disgrace. *We have the power.* We have the power to change the way addiction is perceived. We have the power to change the way addiction is *believed.* We have the power to change the way in which our beloved addicts are judged and treated. Our voices, together and unashamed, are fierce.

We'll know we've succeeded once comfort is baked into bundt cakes—as it is for every other disease.

✳

If my child were dying a slow death from cancer, the world would reach out with comfort. But with addiction, stigma gets in the way.

Stigma and Secrets

Addiction is big; it takes up a lot of space.

I've heard it said there are four lives affected alongside that of every addict. Considering the damage left in my child's wake, that number seems really low, but it indicates that at least half our population suffers with the pain of addiction in some way or another. That's a mighty bundle, equal to every single person from Minnesota to Texas and all the way—east or west—to beach and shining sea.

Well, there's just no room in this crowd for stigma and secrets.

Too many of us are carrying our burden in silence while walking through hell all alone. Too many of us are hiding under shrouds of shame. And too many of us are trying to contort a glaring truth into a camouflaged lie.

Addiction is rowdy and rude and unruly. It is rarely, truly, a secret. It's hard for our friends, neighbors, and coworkers not to notice all the shadowy goings-on. Our lies, avoidance, lowered heads, and averted eyes only perpetuate the notion that addiction is something of a scandal and something to be ashamed of. Something worthy of stigma and secrets. The pent-up beasts need to be released.

*

It's so common, it could be anyone. The trouble is, nobody wants to talk about it. And that makes everything worse.

— RUBY WAX

Natural Order of Things

On the day my youngest child was born, his big brother was eagerly waiting for him. At two-and-a-half years old, he was going to be a faithful friend and special act to follow. And follow, Little Brother did. He followed as his big brother demonstrated how to crawl backward and forward and sideways, how to ride a bike without training wheels, and how to catch fish with just the right flick of the wrist. He watched and learned the art of good aim in the bathroom, of fair play in the backyard, of epic whoppers and burps, and of raw, loyal love. For much of their childhood, my children were Best Brothers. (Well, on most days.) But now, as adults, they are strangers.

Addiction did this.

Instead of fishing—or even fighting—my children no longer know each other. That's what happened once The Addict stole Big Brother's place. One of the many things addiction has destroyed is the natural order of things. Little Brother is now Big Brother's special act to follow. (If only he would.)

Addiction is the destroyer of everything.

Addiction Wants to Win

My child is in control of his disease, no matter what I do (or don't do) to fight against it. Addiction wants to win—*my love is not a failure.*

I do the best I can, but the outcome is not in my control. The desire to use is like the desire to breathe: when it comes to survival, no one and nothing else matters. Addiction wants to win—*my love is not a failure.*

My child and The Addict are in the throes of battle, too, and I know he feels my love. Addiction wants to win—*my love is not a failure.*

Whatever happens next—the best or the worst or somewhere in between—it doesn't mean I didn't love enough or do enough (or love too much or do too much). Addiction wants to win—*my love is not a failure.*

The enemy is strong, the foe is fierce. Addiction wants to win—but my child can be the only victor. *My love is not a failure.*

*

My child has chased everyone away except those The Addict needs in order to survive: the ones who will help his addiction. Not help him.

Why, Oh Why?

Maybe I drove my child to drink, so to speak—maybe he was hurting, mad, or embarrassed of this old gal who so brazenly adored him for the sweet boy he was. Maybe he was insecure and uncomfortable with the process of growing up. Or, maybe he just thought partying with his friends seemed like a fun idea. Whatever his reason for first using drugs and alcohol, my child was also enticed toward the glamorized hole-fillers by popular culture since birth—even though I had taught him to *Just Say No*.

Maybe I should have yelled at my child more (or louder), taken him to church more often, or made sure he watched a little less TV. Maybe I should have hugged him tighter or looser or longer. Or . . . maybe I should decide to set aside the heavy load of *hows* and *whys*. I will never know the answers to these weighty questions, and neither will my child. Maybe what matters now is that I take my steps forward.

Let me give up the need to know WHY things happen as they do. I will never know and constant wondering is constant suffering. — CAROLINE MYSS

Set Us All Free

Once upon a time, I was very ashamed of my child's addiction. I was ashamed of him for what he was doing, and I was ashamed of *me* for being a lousy enough mom to have caused it. I was afraid of what people would think of us, of what they would say. I was afraid of the looks and the whispers, so I kept quiet about what was happening in my family. I hid the shameful secret, dying a little bit inside every day.

Until the day I realized this approach was stupid.

Once *I* shed *my* shame—once I began to say out loud that my child suffers from the disease of addiction— people around me were, for the most part, warm and supportive. They were generous with their kind words, extra hugs, and efforts toward understanding. As for those who weren't supportive, well that just wasn't my problem. The truth set me free. *The truth set us all free.*

*

I could talk until my mouth is dry and my lungs are empty, but still I know that you will never be able to fully understand this pain unless you have to go through it yourself one day. And I sincerely hope that never happens. — ANONYMOUS

A Parent Is Born

When a child tumbles into this world, a parent is born. All soft and hopeful and full of faith. We aren't born to be suspicious—we are meant to trust and believe the children we belong to—but addiction changes that. It pits us against our very nature.

At first, I believed all of my child's stories of wholesome days spent with friends. I believed the excuses for a bad grade (bad teacher) and a sick tummy (bad food). And I believed some very reasonable reasons for a missed curfew here and there. I did not immediately suspect my son when a wine bottle seemed to be missing or when my wallet seemed to be in an odd place in my purse. You see, a parent's belief in a child is strong and sturdy and not easily shaken. A parent's faith in a child is not easily cast aside.

Addiction is cruel, intentionally yanking on the heartstrings of the people who least expect to have their heartstrings yanked. Addiction confuses and abuses what should be the natural ways of parenthood.

*

Never could I have imagined an illness so cruel . . . it broke bonds and hearts and all the rules.

Feels Like War

In the contours of his man-face, I still see my own son. The jaw, the nose, the spacing of his eyes. But I know not to be fooled by the familiar façade: I already know there's somebody else who's living inside. I've been doing battle with this invisible stranger, trying to fight the beast that has wriggled itself underneath my son's skin, but I am so very weary because it often feels like I'm battling against *him*. And sometimes when looking into the face of my child, I'm swayed into feeling like I'm on the wrong side.

I want my son to know whom I'm fighting for.

I want my son to know whom I'm fighting against.

And I want my son to know why.

I want my son to know that I want *him* to win. I want *him* to live. I want *him* to come on home. I want my son to know that even though I'm so very weary from this fight, I won't give up. For *him*.

My child has no idea how hard it is for me to constantly wage war against an invisible enemy—a disease—in what feels like a war against him. He has no idea the toll it takes, hating the addict and loving the son.

The Pull

Once substance use becomes addiction, once The Addict is calling the shots, there's only one thing that matters: Feeding the Beast. There is an insatiable hunger behind the force of addiction—a gnawing, clawing need. Maybe like scrambling to swallow a crushed-glass-filled donut in order to survive.

In the rush *for the rush,* addicts do horrendous things. Criminal things. Unimaginable things. This isn't an *excuse*; it's a *reason.*

Addicts will hurt their own flesh and blood; they will beat their family, cheat them, and then do it again. They will steal from their grandma, from their boss, and from their poor little neighbor. Addicts will deal drugs so they can take drugs—making a deal with the devil. They will risk overdoses and exposure to contagious diseases. And they will get behind the wheel of a car when barely able to stand. Addicts will do anything, *anything,* to get to the next high. They will risk losing their friends, their family, *their life.* If anything makes me understand the force of the pull addicts are facing, it is seeing this.

The mentality and behavior of drug addicts and alcoholics is wholly irrational until you understand that they are completely powerless over their addiction, and unless they have structured help, they have no hope. — RUSSELL BRAND

Nudge from the Nest

I had hoped he would fly. I had expected him to fly. I was *determined* my child would fly when I gave him the nudge (the boot) from the nest. But he didn't. His landing was exactly what you'd expect from a bird gliding through the air without ever flapping its wings.

He could have flown . . . he should have flown. He was born to fly! There's only one reason that my son sank like a stone: he was already an addict, and the disease of addiction had clipped his wings.

Not long before, my son had been a good student with plans for college and a career. The world was his oyster. A pearl just waiting to be plucked. Instead, his potential was squandered. His hopes, his dreams never had a chance to take off.

Yes, I nudged (booted) my baby bird out of the nest only to discover he couldn't fly. This is heartache beyond description.

You never know how strong you are until being strong is your only choice. — BOB MARLEY

Judged

My child became an addict in his teens, lured to drugs and alcohol by a culture that glorifies substance use—the same culture that now, so ignorantly and harshly, passes judgment on him. *And me.*

I am judged for helping, fixing, and pushing (or not helping, fixing, or pushing enough) this sick child of mine who won't be helped or fixed or pushed. I am judged for over-reacting and under-reacting, enabling and letting go. Most hurtful of all, I am judged to be a mother whose love must be somehow flawed.

When my child became an addict, I became the mom of an addict—a role I wasn't prepared for and certainly didn't want. It's a role the whole world seems to have an opinion about, whether they know anything about addiction or not. Whatever I do (or don't do), I am judged to be wrong, but I no longer pay attention to that. I just keep doing what I'm doing, with love.

*

Judge tenderly, if you must. There is usually a side you have not heard, a story you know nothing about, and a battle waged that you are not having to fight. — TRACI LEA LARUSSA

No Tears (Just Jeers)

My son is sick. He suffers from the disease of addiction, a disease that is as debilitating, devastating, and deadly as myriad other diseases. However, in the eyes of many people—maybe even *most* people—he's not a person who is suffering. Rather, he's a pariah.

There's not much empathy directed my son's way. Not much thought given to what it might be like to live in his shoes, in his head, or in his heart. As my child battles his disease—an unimaginable internal fight that he may very well not win—there will be no "wishing-you-wells" directed his way. No get-well-soon cards, no flowers, no balloon bouquets. Instead, he's avoided. Derided. As though he *himself* is the disease. The plague. "You did this to yourself" is the warmest statement of support that he is likely to receive. "You're not sick, you're horrible. You get what you deserve."

No tears are spilled for an addict (except by his family). From those on the outside looking in, there's just the slinging of jeers.

That feeling you get in your stomach, when your heart's broken. It's like all the butterflies just died. — ANONYMOUS

Stolen from Me

My child has been stolen from me. He's even been stolen from himself—The Addict has whisked away my son's very essence. I don't know if I will ever get him back. I know what he's like, the monstrous fiend who took my son away. The Abductor is evil, heartless, selfish, and abusive, with a reputation for spreading anarchy, bondage, devastation, and death.

Thinking about the torture *my child* must endure each and every minute of every day, with every passing year, is torture for *me*. I try not to allow the images to fill my mind (because they kill me)—but they do. Because they slip right on in with the thoughts of my child that fill my mind each and every minute of every day, with every passing year, too.

The Abductor needs my child, my child's body, to survive and will fight to keep him all the way to the bitter end. There is no ransom I can pay. There's no SWAT team on the job. No yellow ribbon tied around a tree.

My child has been stolen from me. There is no end to this hell.

Imagine trying to live without air. Now imagine something worse. — AMY REED

Circus Tent

Right this way, ladies and gentlemen! Step right up! Come one, come all, to the greatest show on earth! We will amaze you. Confound you. Absolutely astound you. You won't believe your eyes.

We have folks jumping through hoops, backward and forward, and contortionists twisting themselves into knots. We have jugglers, gargantuan elephants in the middle of the room that no one seems able to see, and a leopard that can't change its spots. It's amazing! Incredible! The circus is here! It runs non-stop, all through the year!

A ringmaster is here to direct your attention. There are clowns acting funny (kind of teetering about), and tightrope walkers carefully perched on a very fine line. Monkeys are playing games (while teaching their trainers *new* games). And fluffy pink poodles are busily driving about—but, with no sense of boundaries, they can't seem to stay in their lanes. And, of course, there's a lot of flying around without nets.

Right this way! Step right up! Come one, come all! Wait till you see who's holding up this crazy circus tent.

*

I know my boundaries . . . and one day I might just enforce them. — ANONYMOUS

The Land of Tears

I've lived for years in the land of tears—and there's no escape from the sadness.

By day, I retreat, pushing other people away, and I roam the dark house every night. I cry, I pull myself together, and I crawl back into bed. I get up, I fall down, and I try not to drown. I can't eat. I eat too much. I eat away at the fears and worries that are eating away at me. I slap on a smile, I force out a laugh, even on days when I don't make my bed and don't take a bath. I build up a wall, I knock it back down. My love and loyalty get kicked all around. I pretend to be strong. I pretend not to hurt. I try to believe things are going to get better, but too often I don't believe they will. I suffer in silence; I feel so alone.

I've lived for years in the land of tears—and there's no escape from the sadness.

✳

It is such a secret place, the land of tears.

— ANTOINE DE SAINT-EXUPÉRY

Just the Two of Us

Our wedding was beautiful and so were the vows. *Till death do us part* was our promise. But our child's addiction is like a chainsaw, hacking away at our union—cutting apart a bond meant to last forever. It is destroying the foundation on which our family is built.

In the day-to-day survival—during the prolonged hideousness of this fight—we've lost sight of one other. We've lost sight of what matters. We no longer reach out to each other when we hurt. Instead, like wounded animals, we withdraw, trying to heal ourselves as we sit, alone, in dark corners. We snap and growl at each other like beasts. I don't know what happened to the best friends we used to be.

But it is our child's *addiction* we need to fight, not each other. So, like folding away the wings of a kite, I will tuck away the tension between us so it can't catch the wind. No matter what happens during the day, I will say *I love you* when I say goodnight.

May we shine with love, kindness, and encouragement toward ourselves and each other every day. — LYNN DAILEY

The Ghost

There was a ghost living in our house when my youngest child was just a kid, hovering over every bit of his life as he was growing up. The ghost was a character in my youngest son's story; it was just as real as his addicted brother—causing its own form of chaos—and was present even when his brother was not.

Everything that happened in our home and our family made an impression on my youngest child—twice. First, there was the all-too-real drama (and trauma); then there were the hauntings. An arrest here, an overdose there. A drunken car accident, a brother nearly killed. Handcuffs and jail cells, detox and court. Scary phone calls and scary strangers. Scary, out-of-control brother and scary crying mother. Lies, betrayals, and the loss of trust. Love and hate and twisted fate. Everything that happened—both good and bad—had a part in making my youngest son who he is now that he's all grown up.

The ghost living in our house is something my youngest child probably got used to—after all, it was part of the only family he ever knew. The ghost is probably hovering somewhere nearby him, still.

The ghost of my addicted child's mistakes hovered over everything his younger sibling did (and didn't do) . . . and so did his dad and I, skittish and fearful and trying to learn from our own mistakes.

Flowers, Not Weeds

When addiction took hold of my son, it grew and spread like a thick, thorny vine, twisting and turning and choking him tight. But it didn't stop there. It kept right on creeping. It crept and crawled its way into my mind, making *me* sick too. In an *Alice in Wonderland* kind of way, my sickness is a distorted reflection of his sickness. *How sick is that?*

I faded, I weakened. I lost my sense of self. Blamed, judged, and berated, I became consumed by the guilt and negative thoughts heaped on me by both myself and others. My common sense and rational thought became warped.

The truth is, negative thoughts and negative people can't take root in my life if I don't let them. My life is like a garden—what grows here is in my control. Unwelcome seeds may drift in on the wind, and renegade runners may sneak in under the fence, but I can pull out the things I don't want in order to make room for the flowers.

Stop watering the weeds in your life and start watering the flowers. — ANONYMOUS

Green-Eyed Monster

I hate feeling envious. Resentful. I hate that the Green-Eyed Monster occupies even the smallest place in my heart. But it does. This beast is not welcome in my life. I try to keep it squashed down and out of sight, but sometimes it gets loose, popping up out of nowhere, and I have to fight it back down, contain it, before it gets out of hand. I hate that I sometimes feel jealous of happy families, families that haven't been torn apart by addiction—the ones with parents who still seem sane and able to see eye-to-eye, with siblings who are still friends. The ones left untouched by the monsters that commandeer the minds and bodies of unsuspecting children. The families where love hasn't been turned upside down.

Other times—and this is even worse—I'm jealous (just a bit) of the families that have made it to the *other side*. Families that have made it full circle, through the swamp and over the mountains. Recovery families. Happy, healthy, and whole families. I hate the part of me that feels jealous of their victories, but I know another part of me is truly happy. You see, I just ache for a victory like this to also happen in my own family.

It's frustrating to watch everyone else's dreams come true while knowing your own are slipping farther and farther away from becoming reality. — ANONYMOUS

Self-Respect

When my kids used to say, "Mom yelled at me," what they meant was that I had told them to clean their rooms, or to say "please" and "thank you," or to obey some other parental directive they didn't like. To them, this was *yelling* because we just weren't a *yelly* household. So I don't know how my child became comfortable with yelling and swearing *at me* once he became an addict, but he did.

And I let him.

I used to be strong. I had self-respect. I would never have let anyone walk all over me. But with my addicted son, I pretty much rolled out the red carpet. He sneered at me and called me names; he was rude, insulting, and mean. He manipulated me, used me, and abused my love and trust. When he said he hated me, didn't call back, or didn't show up, I pretended it didn't hurt. Instead, I groveled. I was desperate, determined to hang on to the last imaginary thread of our relationship—even if it was abusive.

This is not love—not of the self. Not of anyone.

Unconditional love doesn't mean you have to unconditionally accept bad behaviors. — ANONYMOUS

I Love You

The love I have for you is so much bigger than these three tiny words: *I love you.* My love for you has grown right alongside you, from the day you were born, and will continue to expand in my heart forever. My love is endless, pure, and with no conditions.

Once, when you were little, you stepped on a spiny sea urchin at the beach. You were filled with pain and fear, screaming for my help and kicking away my hands at the same time. You wanted me to help you and hated me for trying—both at the very same time. I love you so much that I will look out for your well-being, whether you like it, or want it, or not.

The love I have for you has nothing to do with expectations. You don't have to do certain things, act in a certain way, believe the things that I believe in, or like the things I like. You don't even have to want my love back.

My love is simple, but it's big.

*

I will love you no matter what. I will love you if you are stupid, if you slip and fall on your face, if you do the wrong thing, if you make mistakes, if you behave like a human being—I will love you no matter. — LEO BUSCAGLIA

As I Was Meant To

Addiction is a disease, but not even the professionals in the field have it all figured out yet—and they aren't trying to figure it out while in a blind panic, running through the fires of hell, with fears and dreams and maternal instincts tripping them up. So, I shouldn't feel like a total failure for having missed so many clues and for not being able to protect my child as I was meant to—but still, sometimes I do.

When my child tumbled into my world, he arrived without an instruction manual, but I did the best job I could as someone with good intentions and no experience. And then I was faced with my son's addiction. I was no match for a disease that's proved slippery enough to evade even the help of experts. So, I shouldn't feel like a total failure for having lost hold of my child—*for not being able to reach my child as I was meant to*—but still, sometimes I do.

✳

Some things in life cannot be fixed. They can only be carried.
— MEGAN DEVINE

Had It All

All or nothing: it doesn't matter. I've talked with people the same age as my son who, as children, were beaten, abandoned, hungry, or lived in the backseat of a car. They grew up with poor schooling, grades, and role models, and made poor choices concerning drugs. Yet, even though they started with seemingly *nothing*, maybe even *less than nothing*, they rose above it all and are now shining like stars.

My son, on the other hand, had it *all*. He was raised without disadvantage. He lived cozily under the wings of an intact family—two parents who loved him, and a brother who (at one time) thought he was pretty great. He had his own room in a nice house, where mom-cooked meals were always on the table. He went to great schools, was raised to follow rules and play fair, and was blessed with good looks, charm, and health. But addiction didn't care about any of that.

Addiction is a monster that takes who it takes. The only way to avoid its random grab is to never take a single puff, sip, or pill in the first place.

You were unsure which pain is worse—the shock of what happened or the ache for what never will. — SIMON VAN BOOY

Connection Rejection

There are some words no mother wants to hear from her child.

"I literally hate you."

I understand it's The Addict—not my child—who spews these hateful words.

"You are an idiot."

I understand it's The Addict—not my child—who rejects all maternal connection.

"Don't contact me."

I understand. Still, I've had to harden my heart to all the hurt. (I hope my heart doesn't shatter.)

"Everyone I know hates you."

But . . . maybe it's *my child*—not The Addict—spewing the hateful words. Maybe, just maybe, the puppet is pulling the strings of the puppeteer. Maybe *my child* is trying to hurt me enough that I'll turn and run away.

"You're just an egg donor to me."

Maybe *my child* wants to chase me away to keep The Addict from hurting me even more. But still, I've had to harden my heart to all the hurt. (I hope my heart doesn't shatter.)

✳

So quit worrying and making your life miserable. Make the cut and finally sever the ties to me if that's what you have to do. (Hate me. I'll make you hate me.)

Path of Most Resistance

It's not that I was lazy. Or blind. Or stupid. It was quite obvious to me that something was wrong. I just didn't want to believe it (and I didn't know what to do with the truth if I did). So I took the path of least resistance, the easy way out. Well, the easiest way out of no easy choices. Compared to butting heads and starting fights with my child and family—compared to having to really face and figure out the big, complicated mess—I took a glide down the slide. I fixed and I coddled, I covered and I coaxed. I bailed out, I bought love, I believed lies. I bribed my child for some peace. This is what I needed to do for a while, until I was ready to stare straight at the mountain before me, admit what it was, and start climbing.

It turns out that the path of most resistance—the uphill battle that I'm still on today—is also *the path provoking the most resistance from The Addict.* So I must be going the right way.

We see what we want to see, especially when we don't want to see it. — ANONYMOUS

Erratic Pinball

I'm bouncing all over the place—a pinball not landed. Family and friends think I have (or think I *should* have) my emotions all sorted out by now, but I don't. One moment I'm doing just fine, moseying along, laughing and having a good time, when, somehow, things get flipped all around and I'm suddenly sobbing and wailing and lying flat on the ground. One moment I'm all happy and content, watching the butterflies in my garden or enjoying a yummy meal with friends, and then the next moment I'm feeling angry and full of turmoil inside—angry for being happy, angry my child is unhappy, angry that I'm such an unpredictable mess. One moment I'm basking in serenity, the peace of having accepted *what is* with grace, and then I find absurdity in that and revolt.

I'm bouncing all over the place like an erratic pinball, no doubt. But it is a journey. My journey. The journey of loving a child with addiction. And some day I might get it all figured out.

For a long time now, I've been careening through the different stages of grief—cluelessness, denial, anger, and acceptance (ha!)—stuck for a while in one stage, zipping past another. An erratic pinball skittering around in a crazy, lonely place.

What's What

With addiction, it's not always clear what you're looking at. Like a chameleon, it takes on the characteristics of so many other things.

Often wildly unpredictable and irresponsible (and, often, just wild), addicts behave in ways that don't make sense. The signs of addiction might imitate some of the less-flattering aspects of teen behavior, or they might look like issues of mental health. It's not always easy to tell what's what.

It's common for people to turn to substances to cope with mental health issues—and those people may, in turn, become addicted. And some people develop mental illness after addiction has already taken hold. Where mental illness and addiction intersect is a fuzzy line, making what is already confusing even more so.

Drugs and alcohol are toxic chemicals—poisons—that trickle in and corrode the brain, and there's no way to tell what behaviors are caused by that damage until the substance use has stopped and enough time has passed for the brain to heal. There's no way to tell until we wait and see what's left.

No parent can tolerate the idea of harm coming to their children, much less the nightmare that is addiction.

— JIM LAPIERRE

Prepared

Even though I've been sliding into the age of fine lines and wrinkles for quite some time now, I still feel a lot like the young person I once was. Not like the wise old owl I thought I'd be by now.

I'd like to say I've figured everything out, but that would be a big lie. I'd like to say I'm prepared for anything, but that would be an even bigger lie. I read, I listen and learn, but I'm not a pro at any task that lands in my path. I'd like to say I have all the answers; instead, I still have a lot of questions (but not even the professionals have all the answers, or even the same answers as each other). The truth is, I've been unprepared for pretty much everything the first time I've first encountered it in my life. But *unprepared* doesn't mean I'm a wilted flower. It just means I need to *get* prepared to fight my son's addiction—better late than never—and do the best I can to avoid messing things up when others are counting on me.

*

That horrifying moment when you're looking for an adult, but you realize you are an adult. So you look around for an older adult, an adultier adult, someone better at adulting than you. — ANONYMOUS

Sticky, Icky Web

A web is such a deceptively delicate thing. All shimmery and silky. But it is strong and sticky enough to capture and hold big things—things that will help to keep the builder of the web alive. Which is, of course, its entire purpose.

With quick wit and lies and tricks of the eyes, an addict collects people to help him. It's so easy to become unwittingly stuck in his trap and stunned senseless. I have been caught in the sticky, icky web too many times to count. Once trapped, I've found myself telling lies, hiding truths, covering things up, and putting out fires—for reasons I can't even explain. I have actually plotted illegal deeds in order to keep my son from getting into trouble, and I have kept secrets from people who could help him. Really.

Time and again, I have tossed myself right into addiction's web—even when my son wasn't around to lure me in.

The best-kept secret about alcoholics and addicts is that they can't survive in their addiction without the cooperation of others. — DEBRA JAY

Equally Loved

One child has brown eyes, the other has blue. One child loves to fish, the other would rather do anything else with his time. One child is an addict, the other is not. Wonderfully unique since birth, each child has traits, talents, and a personality that are a part of the gift I've been given as their mom. I love every bit of each of my boys, with every bit of my heart.

Life requires that I sometimes spend different kinds of time with my children and sometimes show them different kinds of love. But different doesn't mean *out of whack*. It means *in touch*.

Sometimes my undivided attention is divided unevenly between my children; sometimes my attention is needed a bit more over here than over there, or a bit more over there than over here—an ebb and flow tuned to the rhythm of their needs. My *presence* may roll like the waves of an ocean, but the presence of *my love* hangs over the constant tumble of motion like the sky.

The measure of love is to love without measure.

— FRANCIS DE SALES

PART TWO
grow, Grow, GROW

I Will Not Help Kill My Child

My baby grew up to be an addict. There was a time when I believed a mother's love could fix anything, but it can't fix this. For too many years I thought I was helping my child—I thought I was doing my job by keeping him out of trouble and getting him out of trouble and believing him (even when he lied). I tried to keep my child from suffering, because that's what a mother's love does.

I connived. I wheedled. I cried. I begged. And I continued to aid and abet and enable like a champ. I did everything I could to protect my child from himself, until finally I realized it wasn't my son that I was protecting. I was protecting The Addict. Making it easy for The Addict. Giving *The Addict* one more day to further consume my child's body and mind. *I was helping The Addict kill the child I was trying to save.* My motherly love would need to be contorted and redefined. There's nothing about this kind of love that feels good. But I'm not doing it for me.

I will do nothing, ever again, to help The Addict, because, if I do, I have no hope of ever seeing *my child.* I love my child. And it is because I love him that I'm done paying The Addict's ransom.

You can do the impossible, because you have been through the unimaginable. — CHRISTINA RASMUSSEN

Toughest Love of All

Tough-loving an addict has nothing to do with anger or meanness. It doesn't mean that I should be rough and gruff with my son. It doesn't mean I should *turn my back* or *slam the door*.

Instead, it means I will sacrifice what makes me feel good right now for what actually does good for my child in the long term. It means I've come to understand that I can't live his life, make his decisions, or do his work for him. Tough-loving an addict doesn't look the way love is supposed to look—full of give-and-take and trust—because addiction has broken all the rules. But still, it is love.

The expression *tough love* doesn't mean "to be mean." It's called *tough love* because accepting the impossibility of controlling someone else's behavior is *tough to do*. It means, "I love you enough to bear the toughest love of all."

The greatest gift a parent can give a child is unconditional love. As a child wanders and strays, finding his bearings, he needs a sense of absolute love from a parent. There's nothing wrong with tough love, as long as the love is unconditional.

— GEORGE H. W. BUSH

Enablers

I wish I could contain the enabling of everyone around my child, but I don't have enough fingers and toes to plug up the endless leaks in the dam. I can only contain my own enabling, and that is difficult enough; even though I know better, addiction is tricky and sometimes I'm still tricked.

Addiction needs rescuers and fixers and people who will cover things up—*people who will make it easy for the addict to use;* addiction needs rescuers and fixers and people who will cover things up—*people for the addict to use.*

All sorts of people will enable an addict for all sorts of reasons, including good intentions and simple bad judgment. Many people, however, have a twisted understanding of *friendship.* Of *protection.* Of *loyalty.* Of *I've got your back.* But, whenever my child has been broken or close to death, those enablers have disappeared, thankful, I'm sure, the mess wasn't theirs to worry about (if they bothered to give him any thought at all).

The enablers won't lose a single night's sleep if my child dies. But I will.

✳

Most of us enablers are well-intentioned; we act out of kindness, not realizing we've been led to the tip of the skewer by the addict. We try to rescue the addict from himself by fixing his circumstances and kicking his troubles down the road.

Letting Go Is Not the Same as Giving Up

I have to let go of my children. Both of them. That's part of the deal of being a parent: I get to love them and teach them, but I don't get to keep them. I have to set my children free. I have to let them grow up—to be who they were meant to be—and to live their own lives. Like fluttering butterflies, they were born to take flight. If I hold on too tight, I will crush their wings. If I hold on too long, they will smother and die. If I try to flap their wings for them, well, that's just ridiculous (but that doesn't mean I haven't tried). No, I have to let go; I have to believe they can fly. But letting go is not the same as giving up. Letting go is full of hope and possibility. Letting go is giving up the things that belong to my children.

I can do *letting go* . . . but I'm holding their hands with my heart.

*

Sometimes the only way forward is to just Love . . . No judgment, no reaction, no right or wrong. Just a love that says: I know who you are, and I trust you to find your way.

— JULIE PARKER

A Love Letter to Parents

(by Jason Branham)

—THE TRUTH FROM ANOTHER MOTHER'S CHILD—

I know you've gone over every single thing trying to figure out what you could have done to prevent me from becoming an addict. But you couldn't have loved me more, watched over me more (or less), cooked more dinners, or spent more time with me. It wasn't that I didn't have the right toys or clothes, car or education, and it wasn't that you didn't do your best to give me a happy childhood. The truth is this: I drank and did drugs not because you made bad choices, but because I made bad choices.

One cold December morning, you said: "I love you, but you can't live here anymore and keep using. I will not watch you die." You handed me a bag of sandwiches and that was it. You loved me enough to say "no more." I want you to know that I stayed gone because I cared so much that I couldn't bear for you to see me the way I was.

Thank you for loving me no matter what, and for having faith that eventually I would love myself, too. Please find peace in knowing that my addiction was not your fault.

It's not just other people we need to forgive. We also need to forgive ourselves. For all the things we didn't do. All the things we should have done. — MITCH ALBOM

Not All Figured Out

When my boys were growing up, they could sometimes play me like a fiddle. Three bedtime stories instead of one; ice cream instead of an apple; a new puppy; a later curfew; the car on a weeknight. I didn't always know when I was being played, and I didn't always know if what I was doing was right, but usually the decisions—and the consequences—of giving in (or not) weren't a big deal.

At least, not compared to the fallout of the bigger and better and badder manipulations of an addict. I still don't always know if I'm being played, and I don't always know if what I'm doing is right, *but the decisions—and the consequences—of giving in (or not) are usually excruciatingly painful and enormous.*

Five dollars for food? (What if he's hungry?) Five hundred dollars for rent? (What if he's broke because he spent all his money buying drugs?) Use my car for a job interview? (What if he drinks and drives instead?) Kick him out of the house if he steals? From me? From his brother? (What if he becomes homeless?) Do I say yes? No? I don't always know.

*

I think we've got this parenting gig nailed . . . said no parent ever. — LISA MALTBY

Un-abling

It is not *helping* my child if I do things for him that he can (and should) do for himself. Instead, by diminishing expectations, I diminish his capabilities. I am *un-abling*.

Un-abling means that I am helping to make the son I am "helping" unable to manage his task—or his life—on his own. It is crossing boundaries, reducing responsibilities, removing consequences, and cheating him of things adults need to learn in order to live (and love) life on their own. It's providing an escape hatch from the realities of life.

So, I will not give in, hand out, set up, or fix up my child's messes and catastrophes until I am, inevitably, unable to enable. (Or unwilling. Or burned out.) I will not help to leave my child so *un-abled* that he is unable to handle the business of running whatever is left of his life—after he's endured a lifetime of my un-abling. (What happens to my child if he never learns how to rescue himself?) All I can (and should) do is help him to get the help he needs to help himself. That, *and love him.*

If he sneezes, I'm not the one who should leap for a tissue. And I'm not the one who should want to.

Puppets

Although his nose doesn't grow when he lies, I feel like maybe it should. My son is a whole lot like Pinocchio, except this is real life, and *addiction* is the puppeteer pulling his strings and controlling his every move. Addiction is making him say and do and think things he wouldn't normally say or think or do.

My son is not the only puppet on a string. I am also manipulated by unseen hands. Addiction may be toying with my son, but The Addict toys with me. I am fooled into saying, doing, and thinking things I wouldn't normally say or think or do. And, even while I'm being jerked around by The Addict, I catch myself trying to pull my son's strings. What a tangle.

I know that I cannot control my son. Yet that doesn't always stop me from trying to make him say, do, and think the things I think he needs to say and do and think to free himself from addiction. It may seem impossible to tell who is controlling whom, but there is only one puppet master—addiction—and it is controlling the whole show.

✳

My child is not a marionette I can control with words or wishful thinking. My actions are not his actions. My pulling the strings isn't the same thing as him doing the work. I need to clip the strings.

The Same Shadow

Somewhere in there is my son. I know he's still there. Somewhere beneath, behind, within The Addict that is wearing his face. Yes, somewhere in there is my sweet child, *the child I love.* But The Addict, who looks like my child, is a mean and vicious tormentor—a kidnapper of souls who keeps my son hostage—and I hate him.

Somewhere in there is my child, still looking at me and listening to me, his mom. He sees me and hears me cheering for him to make it to the other side. He knows that I miss him and want him back. He knows I haven't slammed the door on him (just The Addict). He knows that I know he is not his addiction—that he is more than his addiction. That *he* was *him* before his addiction. And that *he* can *be him* again.

Somewhere in there is my child, and he's depending on the bond we share—the bond he knows can never be broken. I will not let him down. My child and The Addict may share the same shadow, but they will not share my love.

✳

So, Addiction: GO TO HELL. There will be times when I'm tired or stupid or tricked. And there will be times when I don't like this son of mine. But don't be fooled. I'm full of love for him. It may not look the way love is supposed to, but my love is strong and it is forever.

A Cactus

Addiction is a disease, and like other diseases, it can be managed by following a specific treatment plan. But from where I sit, that's where the similarities end.

With addiction, I don't get to sit at my child's bedside, giving comfort, holding his hand while we battle his disease together. There is no relationship left between us—addiction has made sure of that. Addiction twists, uses, and manipulates everyone in its path. It will lie and cheat and steal. It will turn mean and violent. And it will rip families apart by turning people against one another—mother against father, sister against brother. Addiction deeply embeds its thorns into the very same brain that must be healthy to do what it takes to heal. And, stuck to the ugly sisters of stigma and shame, it is looked upon as a choice or a crime—so, with addiction, no one ever sends flowers.

Addiction has changed the very essence of my son. I'm never certain if I'm talking to my child or the addict; whose eyes am I looking into, and whose eyes are looking back? From where I sit, addiction is a particularly prickly disease, unlike any other.

Being negative only makes a difficult journey more difficult. You may be given a cactus, but you don't have to sit on it.

— JOYCE MEYER

Conundrum

Addicts need *treatment* for their disease, not time behind bars, but addicts often spend a lot of time in criminal territory, so this presents a real conundrum.

Ideally, the addict would recognize his disease and voluntarily enter long-term inpatient addiction treatment before committing any crimes, fully embrace recovery, and be done. But, from what I have seen, that's not usually how things go. From my viewpoint, things go more like this: The addict doesn't think he has a problem even though he's committed crimes and been arrested. He cannot be convinced to go into treatment—and if he's an adult, he can't be forced to go—so he's free to commit more crimes, to continue to get arrested, and to become more deeply addicted. Finally, possibly, before death or some other hideously irreversible destruction, the addict is forced or coerced into treatment, but he walks out the door in a short time, free, again, to steal or deal (or overdose or die) or get re-arrested and land back in jail. Without getting treatment for his disease.

The biggest crime in this conundrum is that there are no easy answers.

*

Acceptance is not submission; it is acknowledgment of the facts of a situation. Then deciding what you're going to do about it. — KATHLEEN CASEY THEISEN

Twenty-Eight Days

Twenty-eight isn't a magic number. It doesn't have anything to do with optimum results. Instead, the typical twenty-eight-day stint in addiction treatment is determined by insurance companies. Twenty-eight days isn't enough time for the brain to heal—not after years of abuse. It's not enough time for priorities to realign and connections to reconnect, or for rebuilding and rediscovering lifestyles and relationships (and self). Twenty-eight days isn't enough time to learn how to live a life that is abstinent—to learn how to use all the tools—to learn how to un-trigger triggers, break habits, curb cravings, and tamp down unbidden thoughts. Twenty-eight days is just not enough time for the addict to change and stabilize all of the things that need changing and stabilizing—which is pretty much every single thing in the addict's life. It's not even enough time for the addict to process what's happening in the present, much less how to process the past and the future.

Addiction treatment needs to be given enough time to work, the first time, helping to lessen the chance of relapses and revolving doors. Twenty-eight days just isn't enough.

*

Recovery is a process. It takes time, it takes patience, it takes everything you've got. — ANONYMOUS

"Addict" Is Not a Bad Word

My child is not a junkie, druggie, stoner, dope-head, burnout, or freak. These are ugly words slapped onto a disease that people don't understand. But my child *is* an addict.

"Addict" is not a bad word. It's a misunderstood word. It doesn't mean *bad person* or *weak person*. Nor does it mean *person who chooses to party all day*. The word "addict" is a logical derivative of the word *addiction*, originating from the Latin word *addictus*, which means *slave*. "Addict" means: *A person bound as a slave to the disease of addiction*. My child *is* an addict, but that is nothing to be ashamed of and that one word does not define him any more than any of his other traits. Being an addict is just one part of the whole package.

No, "addict" is not a bad word, but the stigma behind the word is shameful and needs to be changed. Once addiction is understood as a disease—once the misconceptions are cleared up—perceptions will change and the stigma associated with the word will diminish. This is what matters. Let's educate, not complicate. One word. One disease. One understanding.

*

Sometimes the questions are complicated and the answers are simple. — DR. SEUSS

Not a Free Pass

The designation of addiction as a disease does not in any way excuse the addict from responsibility; it is not a free pass. It is not a reason to roll over and give up. It is not an excuse for unfettered drug use. In fact, recognition of addiction as a disease establishes expectation and hope; within the addict's reach is a very doable plan. As with many other serious diseases, diagnosis requires adherence to a treatment plan—and, also like many other serious diseases, recovery, though difficult, is attainable.

There's a widely held belief that addicts are bad people, but the truth is, addiction is not an issue of moral judgment. Addiction has nothing whatsoever to do with whether a person is nice, the quality of their character, or the strength of their will. Most addiction begins in adolescence, before a person's brain is fully developed and while strongly enticed by popular culture. It is not a choice. Addiction is forever—there is no cure—it cannot simply be stuffed back in the bottle or under the rug. It's a chronic disease and relapse is likely—because doing what is needed to stay in recovery happens one day at a time and is hard work.

*

Addiction is a chronic, often relapsing brain disease. . . Although the initial decision to take drugs is voluntary for most people, the brain changes that occur over time challenge an addicted person's self-control and hamper his or her ability to resist intense impulses to take drugs.

— NATIONAL COUNCIL ON ALCOHOLISM
AND DRUG DEPENDENCE

Don't Wait Until It's Too Late

If I wait until he's dead—until after addiction has killed him—if I wait until I'm writing my son's obituary to tell the truth of his life—then I've done nothing to help, or to help others to help, keep him alive.

If I wait until he's dead to talk about his addiction—because of shame, embarrassment, false pride, or Grandma's desire to not air dirty laundry, then I've put what *doesn't* matter before what *does* matter, and put those who don't have their lives on the line before the one who does: *my son*. If I wait until he's dead—out of my own fear or pressure from *The Addict*—then The Addict will win the war without even having to fight a battle. If I wait until he's dead, just a carcass, killed by the same drugs or alcohol destroying his life while alive, then I've let my child down. I've not let him see me stand up to protect him, to open eyes and hearts and minds, to help people to understand him. I must speak out, before it's too late.

Do you have the patience to wait till your mud settles and the water is clear? Can you remain unmoving till the right action arises by itself? — LAO TZU

Bestness

Attitude determines the tone, which foretells the outcome—both in my interactions with others and within my very own head. For example, if a waiter happens to bring me the wrong order, and I say, *"Thanks a lot,"* but *my tone* implies "You idiot," chances are the rest of my meal will not turn out as planned. My bad attitude won't have done anybody any good. Self-sabotage is a beast to be tamed.

"I'm doing the best I can," I might say to myself or to friends. Depending on my attitude, my tone, these words might mean: "This is hard. It's not working. I've tried, but this is all I can do. I'll keep doing what I'm doing, but don't expect more from me. I'm tired." The outcome? Likely *not* my best.

With a little adjustment, a little taming of the self-sabotaging beast, those exact same words, *"I'm doing the best I can,"* might mean something very different: "I tried, and when that attempt didn't work, I tried again, and then I tried something different. I will keep trying new ways and will not give up until I figure out this thing that's got me stuck." When I say, *"I'm doing the best I can,"* what I'm saying is "I choose to choose bestness."

✳

Do the best you can until you know better. Then when you know better, do better. — MAYA ANGELOU

Good for the Gander

I want my son to love himself (and me) enough to give up the things he loves more than anything else: drugs and alcohol. I want him to give them up so he can live a long and healthy life—live it to the fullest—and hopefully spend some of it with me. I want him to give up the things that are making him sick, the things that will also make him sick to give up. I want him to sacrifice what he so desperately wants right now for what I know will be a battle he'll have to fight forever.

I want all of that from him . . . and for him. Real work. Real pain. Real commitment. To get better. To be better. And I want to get better, be better, too. I want to show that I understand real sacrifice and pain. I want to prove to my son that I can bite off and chew the same tough stuff that I expect him to. I want my talk to have walked the walk. Not just for him to see, but because the self-improvement that's good for him is also good for me. What's good for the goose is good for the gander. I'm committed to working on improving me.

✳

It is not fair to ask of others what you are not willing to do yourself. — ELEANOR ROOSEVELT

Wallowing

Not at all concerned that it (and he) is a big, old muddy mess, a pig will wallow around in a puddle of mud simply because it feels good. I have done this too. Not literally, of course. Not in the mud. But I have wallowed in a big, old puddle of self-pity and misery. And it's been quite a mess.

All muddled up in my misery, I felt a connection with my son—and it was something I had to hang on to because it was the only connection I had. The boo-hoos and the moping, the flopping and flailing, the blubbering and sobbing and wailing were a demonstration of love; the louder it was, the more devoted I was. The more reclusive I was, the more loyal I felt myself to be. Really. Somehow I believed this.

Clinging to misery is not a demonstration of the strength of my love. It's an excuse for not moving forward.

Embracing my strength is not a weakness.

We either make ourselves miserable or we make ourselves strong. The amount of work is the same.

— CARLOS CASTANEDA

No Place to Go

Love is supposed to flit about, here and there. Happily. And lightly. It's also supposed to have a place to land. Love is supposed to reach out and check in: *How's the job? How's your life? Wanna do lunch? Go for a walk? Wanna talk? Do you need help with this or that? Happy Birthday! Here's a birthday cake, some presents, birthday wishes, a party hat.* Yes, love is supposed to flit about, here and there, doing all these things, and more.

With addiction, love has no place to go. No place to land. My love, as a mother, has become untethered. So, in trying to make things right in my maternal world, I fuss, fix, and fume instead—forcing and faking a two-way relationship. I butt in and argue and wheel and deal and wheedle and enable and un-able and whine and beg. Love is supposed to flit about, here and there. Happily. And lightly. But there's nowhere for my love to go. Or land. And so, I ache.

Grief is just love with no place to go. — JAMIE ANDERSON

Zip It

Not every thought needs to become a spoken word. Not every feeling needs to become an action. *Sometimes I need to just keep quiet.* If my words will seem harsh— if they will ridicule, judge, or critique—I won't say them. If they will be unkind, I will be kind and leave them unsaid. If I have an opinion (or advice) that hasn't been asked for, I will keep it to myself. If it's not an objective fact, I won't present it; if it's not a truth, I won't spread it; if it's not mine to discuss, I won't discuss it. If I don't *want* to know or don't *need* to know—and if I *cannot* or should not do anything about it—then I will not ask about it. If I'm mad, I don't need to yell it; if I'm resentful, I don't need to prove it; if I'm hurting, I don't need to hurt someone back. I need to think before I speak or act. Mostly, I just need to *zip it*.

A closed mouth gathers no foot. — ANONYMOUS

Accidental Addict

Every addict is an *accidental* addict; no person on this earth becomes an addict on purpose. Not the person shooting heroin in a back room. Not the person smoking pot behind school at a young age. Not the high school junior doing shots of tequila with friends after a ball game on a Friday night. Not the person having a glass of wine after dinner. And not the person popping pills for pain after a slip on the ice and a broken shoulder: a prescription doesn't make someone's addiction more accidental than any other.

The accidental addict doesn't have a particular look or set of lifestyle ingredients — no particular skin, hair, or eye color. No particular size to their houses or wallets. And addiction doesn't happen to everyone who takes a sip or pill, although it is a possibility for anyone who opens Pandora's box.

Nobody thinks addiction will happen to them, but accidents happen. It might be better to say that all the people who've tried drugs or alcohol who *didn't* become addicts are *accidental non-addicts*.

Addiction is addiction is addiction. — DR. NORA VOLKOW

Recovery All Around

As a mom, I get to pour love over my children from the moment they're born—until, one day, they are full to the brim and fortified enough to face the world on their own. *I get to love my children to let them go.* It's the way nature intended things. But there's nothing natural about what addiction has done to my relationship with my son, so letting go hasn't looked the way it's supposed to. Instead, it looks like a horrible mess. The disease that made my child sick has made me sick too; contagious, like an infection, it has festered and spread.

Instead of letting go of this adult child of mine, I snoop and stalk and try to out-manipulate his manipulations. I try to keep from spilling secrets and to keep all those secrets in a straight line. I do everything and anything to make things right, yet things stay so very wrong. I need help in figuring out how I'm supposed to love and let go in this world of addiction. I need help in figuring out how to let go of my son. I need to find a recovery of my own—for his sake, and mine.

*

Recovery doesn't happen in a vacuum; when the addict leaves treatment, they come back to the real world, which includes their families. Treat us all, and the stigma around addiction is destroyed and all the issues surrounding addiction can be addressed with understanding and compassion.

— NADINE HORTON

Boundaries

Fences are built to keep valuable things safe—to keep children and pets from escaping or running headlong into danger. Roadways have painted lines to keep cars in their own lane, and homes have signs to keep interlopers away. Boundaries keep things in place, keep things *just so*. Keep problems from popping up. Keep things under control. Boundaries are a necessity.

Boundaries don't need to be wrapped in barbed wire or topped with shards of glass or constructed of three-foot-thick blocks of concrete. Boundaries don't need to be hostile. Or harsh. Boundaries can also be neatly trimmed hedges or flower gardens or silken lengths of rope. Boundaries can be passive. Quiet. They don't have to push and shove—sometimes, they're just there. A definition of space. A reminder not to cross.

Boundaries are what I make of them. They are what I need them to be. To protect myself and others. Boundaries are a necessity.

Boundaries, boundaries, boundaries. Don't leave home without them. — JEFF BROWN

A Victor, Not a Victim

I must *empower* without pitying. I must encourage a *victor,* not a victim. My child must be allowed to fall down if he's going to learn how to pick himself up. Instinctively, I knew this when he was little. I knew this when I let go of his hand so he could take his first steps, and when I let go of his bike the first time he rode without training wheels. It hurt my heart. But letting him fall down is even harder now that he's bigger—it hurts even more because the falls are bigger. Still, I must allow him to learn and live and manage his own life.

I will not hover about and cry out at every stumble. Every mistake. I will not tell my son he is too sick, weak, or incapable. Instead, I will nurture the idea of limitless potential. I will remember the story of parents whose child was born without any limbs and follow their example: not only has their child grown to manage his daily routine . . . he has also mastered the ability to swim, ski, and paint. This boy's parents believed he could do anything. And he did.

I will give my son the dignity and privilege of owning his own life.

*

But darling, in the end, you have to be your own hidden hero, because everyone is busy trying to save themselves.

— ANONYMOUS

Déjà Vu

I've heard it all before. I know—more or less—what the addict is going to say before he even says it. I know the reason for losing his job. The reason for losing his phone, his wallet, his rent money. (And for losing me.)

I know who's to blame for something, anything, everything: his horrible boss, horrible girlfriend, horrible roommate, horrible neighbor, horrible landlord. (And me.) I know the details of the stories for why he is late, or didn't get the message, or got lost. I know all about the corrupt people messing around with his life: the corrupt police, the corrupt judge, and the corrupt people who support the other corrupt people. (And me.)

I know the promises by heart—the promises that are *for real this time*—the ones about staying sober, going into treatment, being honest, or paying back an old debt. I know too well the empty apologies for stealing, misleading, manipulating, or using, or for not showing up. Yes, I've heard it all before. But from now on, I won't accept the same old untruths. My approach will be different. From now on I'll call *Bull!*

✳

Déjà Moo: When you know you've experienced this bull$!# before.* — ANONYMOUS

Presence

Better than a diamond, a fancy new gadget, or any present that can be put into a box and tied up with a bow, is the gift of *presence*.

In the chaos of addiction, however, in the swamp of pervasive pain, I often feel overwhelmed, unable to take any more or to face any more, and so I shuffle off to my own corner and hide. I feel unable to tackle the niceties of time and togetherness. I let important things slide.

I am part of a unit—a marriage, a family, a team—and my loved ones rely on me to love them enough to not leave them stranded. We all hurt. But our personal hurt does not serve as permission to hurt everyone else even more. Disengaged, distant—there, *but not all there*—these bailouts create a big black hole for wives and husbands and children to fall into, one by one. Gone. I won't let that happen. I will give my family what they need and deserve: all of me. I will share my presence. The best present of all.

If you don't make the time to work on creating the life you want, you're eventually going to be forced to spend a lot of time dealing with a life you don't want. — KEVIN NGO

Read the Signs

Are my actions helping this child I'm trying so hard not to hurt? Or are they actually hurting this child I'm trying to help? Who are my actions actually *serving*? My child? The Addict? Or, possibly, are my actions just serving *me*?

I need to take a hard look, read the signs, and pay attention to the answers—even if the signs and answers may not be what I want them to be. Or if they mean I must do things differently than I'm doing them now. *Or if they mean helping him means hurting me.*

Addiction takes things to a whole new level, but I've had plenty of experience with boys who don't want—or don't like—to do something that is in their best interest. A little (or big) tantrum has never scared me.

I've discovered that if *The Addict* is happy with my help, then I'm probably enabling. If The Addict says he hates me and stomps out of the room, then I'm probably helping *the child,* whom I love.

✳

The worst thing about enabling is that it almost always feels like the right thing to do. We see someone we love suffering and are drawn to relieve their pain. In the context of addiction, protecting a person from the natural consequences of their actions is, without question, hurting them.

— JIM LAPIERRE

Fight the Right Enemy

Every journey, every nightmare, is different. Each one of us is fighting our own unique fight. Alone or together, we are each trying to cope with the disease of addiction that has so viciously attacked our lives. Overwhelmed by a flood of mixed emotions, mixed messages, and mixed results, we often think we're doing things all wrong, but there's never only one way to do things right. What worked (or didn't work) for you or me may (or may not) save (or not save) the life of someone else's beloved addict.

Let's fight the right enemy—the disease—not the people who have different opinions and experiences. Let's help one another survive instead of helping the disease survive. Let's channel our pain into words that build one another up, instead of cutting one another off at the knees.

Let us never forget that it is the *disease* with which we do battle—not the addicts consumed by the disease and not the people who love them. Let us fill the lives riddled by addiction with compassion and understanding.

Sometimes we need to look hard at a person and remember that he is doing the best he can. He's trying to find his way, that's all. — ON GOLDEN POND

Letting Go of the Silence

Addiction's best friends are shame and silence—without them, addiction couldn't survive. They play together so nicely, hanging out deep in the shadows. A tight-knit gang of bullies, they've been left to rule through intimidation for too long. Addiction, shame, and silence—this trio with power.

Many times, out of fear, I've kept addiction's secrets— fear of blame, fear of my failures being exposed, fear of embarrassment and disgrace. But now I see that was stupid; my silence and shame only help The Addict to succeed at killing my son. So, I will no longer be silent. Or ashamed.

The best gift I can give *The Addict* is to keep quiet—to keep addiction hidden away in the dark. But the best gift I can give *my child* is to talk about addiction. To bring addiction out into the light, to foster understanding and change. To change the way people look at my son. To change the way they interact with and treat him.

Maybe *letting go with love* means *letting go of the silence.*

Stigma's power lies in silence. The silence that persists when discussion and action should be taking place.

— M. B. DALLOCCHIO

Nothing Is Something

Something has presence. It is big. Important. The world, a book, a mountain, a hug—all of these are *something*. You can put your hands on (or around) *something*. Put your feet on it. Touch it. Walk on it. You can feel *something* with your fingertips. Or feel it in your heart.

Nothing is something too. It may seem like air. Like an empty space. A hole. But when *nothing* is filled with the biggest something of all—love—then nothing, too, is something that can be felt with the heart. It becomes substantial. It has heft. It hangs somewhere between hope and faith. It is the space between my hand and yours as you reach out to steer your own life.

Sometimes love means doing nothing rather than doing something. All I can do now is love you, my son— but I know how big of a something that really is.

I don't want you to save me. I want you to stand by my side as I save myself. — SUSHIL SINGH

Worse—or Not Worse

I can't make my son *better*. I can't make his addiction *better*. I can't make our family *better*. And I can't make me *better*. I know because I've tried. Addiction has devastated my family and everyone in it. It has robbed us of relationships and bonds, old memories and new memories, as well as dreams and aspirations. Our lives are punched with hatefulness and holes. Some things cannot be unseen, unheard, unsaid, or undone, and addiction continually spews out things that are immensely destructive. I can never make things *better*—just as I cannot shove lava and ash back into a volcano that has erupted.

But, I can make things *not worse*. I can make new things—good things—grow amongst the mess. I can adapt and learn and share and spread goodness to make up for all the badness. And I can certainly avoid making things *worse* by not getting sucked into The Addict's chaos and drama, or creating additional chaos and drama of my own. It comes down to this: I can make things *worse* or I can make things *not worse*. This is what I can control.

No matter how bad things are, you can always make things worse. — RANDY PAUSCH

The Weakest Link

Every addict has one. (Or two.) Like a rabbit's foot or talisman that the addict carries in his pocket, the *weakest link* is the person who makes things easy for the addict—the addict's lucky day. The weakest link is the addict's jackpot.

It's not hard for the addict to find someone to fill the position of weakest link, someone he can use to keep his addiction going. The person who believes everything the addict says. Who sees the addict as a victim. Who "helps" because it feels good even if it doesn't really do the addict any good at all. The weakest link is the person who doesn't understand what helping really means; who knows best and knows it all; who helps the addict to self-destruct. The weakest link is the person the addict finds he can most easily manipulate, the person who can be most easily broken. There's one in every crowd.

Families and friends—we are interconnected through life. A daisy chain, only stronger. But the addict chips away—chip, chip, chip—hunting for the weakest link. Every addict finds one. (Or two.)

Rescuing someone who is actively practicing addiction of some kind is enabling. It is dysfunctional because it supports the person in continuing to practice their addiction.... Helping someone to continue to self-destruct is not support; it is codependency. It is also not loving. — ROBERT BURNEY

The Strongest Link

Every family has one. (And, occasionally, two.) The *strongest link* is the addict's nemesis. A sharp thorn in the addict's side. From the addict's perspective, the *strongest link* stops good things from happening.

It's not hard for the addict to recognize the strongest link, the person he cannot manipulate into helping his addiction to thrive. The strongest link is the person who doesn't believe a word the addict says. Who doesn't see the addict as a victim, but as a victor who can fight the fight. Who doesn't "help" in ways that might feel good but don't do the addict any good at all. The strongest link is the person who does everything possible to thwart the addict; who tries to stop the addict from killing the child within; who won't help the addict to self-destruct. The strongest link is the person the addict finds he cannot dupe and use, the person who stands strong against the disease.

Families and friends—we are interconnected through life. A daisy chain, only stronger. The addict doesn't like unity and strength, and despises the strongest link, but, thankfully, every family has one. (And, occasionally, two.)

Addicts instinctively know which family member has the greatest capacity to threaten their addiction. — DEBRA JAY

Lies

Addicts lie. About everything. All the time. To anyone. They lie to Mom and Dad, Grandma, the boss, police, and doctors. Addicts carry such a bundle of lies, of all shapes and sizes, they can't keep them neatly contained.

I don't always know when the addict is lying; a good lie might fly right over my head. Sometimes I *suspect* I'm looking at a lie, so I step back and try to make sense of the things not adding up all around me. Other times, a lie is a big fat whopper, impossible not to see, but *not* impossible to ignore (because, you see, I don't always want to start a fight). The lies come pouring in, unwelcome and uninvited, like a dump truck dropping rubbish on top of my head. I feel like a participant in the lies just by being an innocent bystander. And I feel like I am validating the lies—feeding the addict—if the addict *believes* that I believe the lies.

But, I don't need to go seeking *more* trouble with lies. I don't need to go snooping around, asking the addict questions, when I'm pretty sure I will be told things that aren't true. The lies don't need to be given a stage.

✳

Ask no questions and you'll be told no lies.

— CHARLES DICKENS

Changing Others

People ask why I don't make my adult son go to addiction treatment again, and why I didn't make him stay in treatment all the times before. They wonder why I don't stop him from using drugs and why I don't get him to turn his life around. People seem to think I have the power to change my son, the addict, but I don't.

It's hard enough to muster up enough power to make even small changes within myself. Think *New Year's Resolution,* and you'll know what I mean. I want to walk every day. I want to lose a bunch of pounds; I really do. But my own bad habits are hard to change. Nagging doesn't work. If someone suggests I should lose a few pounds—for my own health—I feel judged and unacceptable as I am. It doesn't make me want to start a diet; it makes me want to go eat a bowl of ice cream. (I'm not prickly by nature, so I think this is *human nature.*)

My son knows what he needs to do and will make changes when he's ready to change. Or not. And no one can change that.

Consider how hard it is to change yourself and you'll understand what little chance you have in trying to change others.
— JACOB M. BRAUDE

Sanity, Perspective, and Wisdom

Battle-worn and weary, parents of addicts are a sad and lonely lot. But addiction is too complicated—too colossal—for us to face, and fight, without help. None of us started out prepared for this journey, but we are not alone. In groups big and small across the country and world, parents are supporting other parents. (I think this may be how we survive.)

Heard. That's what I feel when I sit in a room full of other moms and dads who know what I think and feel—what I have seen and done (and not done)—without even opening my mouth. They understand the love, the fears, and even the feelings and thoughts I've had but am not proud of. These moms and dads share their successes and mistakes and failures, shining a light for me on my own path. What I find is my sanity, some much-needed perspective, and a healthy dose of wisdom. I find the strength to fight on.

If the battle against addiction is a war of strength and wit, I will surround myself with the people who will help me to become stronger. And wiser.

I alone can do it. But I can't do it alone. — ANONYMOUS

Vibes

Like bees in the garden, floating from flower to flower, my maternal instincts are always humming. Always meandering about. Always quietly abuzz. Except when they're screeching like the five alarms for a fire—and since my child is an addict, my maternal instincts are often on high alert.

My instincts help out when my eyes and ears alone aren't quite enough for the job of determining whether my kids are all right. My instincts help in sorting out when something is wrong, or *really* wrong, and I have learned to listen to—and trust—them.

I have known something is wrong by looking at the back of my child's head, or by hearing the rustle of covers at night, or by listening to a particular sort of silence. If a suspicion or uneasy feeling is niggling at my mind—if I feel like something is wrong—it probably is. It's better for me to *react* than it is to squash down the vibes and regret it later. It's better to say, "I'm sorry if it seems like I overreacted, but I care about you," than it is to say, "I'm sorry I didn't show you that I care."

Vibes speak louder than words. — ANONYMOUS

Love and Hate

Yin and yang. Two sides of the moon. Two musical notes that are harmoniously discordant. I love my child. My love for him fills my heart. But there are times when I hate him with equal force. Dark and bright. Heavy and light. The rival emotions are all crowded together in the center of my being, a knotted jumble that I can't figure out.

I love my son so much that I hate him for hurting himself, for putting himself in harm's way. Once, when my son was little, he ran out into the street, into the path of an oncoming car. In terror, I snatched him from certain death, hugging him tightly—and then I wanted to kill him. A clashing tangle of feelings, duking it out. This is how my heart feels most of the time now that my son is grown, consumed by The Addict.

I know that I don't ever really hate my son; I know it's *the things he's doing* that I hate, not him. I know that I love *my son* and hate *his addiction*. And I know that love and hate can somehow both fit together under the same hat.

✳

I hate you and then I love you. It's like I want to throw you off a cliff, then rush to the bottom to catch you. — ANONYMOUS

Please Don't Enable Me: A Letter

(by Audrey Porter)

I am an addict. My success in staying clean demands that you accept the harsh reality that I, your child, can and will look you straight in the eye and lie. I will go to extreme lengths to get drugs. You must say *no* to me. No cash, no gift cards, no to anything that can be sold or traded. I need you to stand firm; I've got scheming down to an art. Should I use again, I will die; if I relapse, it must not be with your money or while living in your home. I may get angry, but someday I'll thank you. I need you to resist the urge to pick up pieces for me as I rebuild my life. I must do the work myself, over time.

Please help me by stepping out of my path to recovery, and no longer allow me to manipulate your love for me into enabling. You'll be gifting me the opportunity to find the true beauty of life that's under the years of chaos I created. Each time you rescue me from the natural consequences of my addiction, you hinder my growth, although I know you've done this out of love.

✳

Once the enabling stops, the recovery is given the opportunity to start. — ANONYMOUS

No

Just Say No. Once the motto for our nation's antidrug crusade, this catchphrase was born from the desire to help our children avoid being snagged by the nefarious net of addiction. I dutifully taught my child to *Just Say No* to drugs, and he promised that he would, but when actually faced with the situation, he said *yes.* A snappy slogan for a very complex problem, *Just Say No* isn't a solution, but it does have its place. It is a starting point. And, *no* is a word everyone needs to be comfortable using. It's also, very often, the correct answer to give to an addict.

No is a complete answer. No explanation is required. *No, no, no.* I will practice it. I will get used to the feel of *no* rolling off my tongue: "*No,* I won't loan you money. *No,* I won't pay your rent." I will write myself little notes, strength-building reminders, keeping them handy for when I need to say *no* without getting into a brouhaha.

It's okay to say *no.* (I don't think I need to write anything here about how it's okay to say *yes.*)

✳

"Oh honey, I would, but I don't want to."

— KAREN, *WILL & GRACE*

Two Boys

Two boys. Born two years apart. They grew up in the same house, these two boys. They were raised by the same parents—and they both had to endure those same parents' myriad quirks and idiosyncrasies. They grew from the same foundation, under the same rules, and were rained upon by the same shower of love. Other than where they happened to land in the chronological order of their family—benefitting, or not, from the parental evolution of experience—the world from which they sprouted was the same.

Two boys. Born two years apart. They walked the same ground, these two boys, but they each wore their own pair of boots. They began their journeys as two distinctly different individuals, blessing their family, their community, their world, with their own personalities, sensitivities, and strengths, each carrying a genetic makeup uniquely their own. They took different paths, *making their own paths*—as it should be—following dreams, making choices, rubbing elbows with different people and different experiences, developing unique perceptions and talents and vulnerabilities.

Two boys. Born two years apart. One became an addict, the other did not.

✳

Both of my boys set sail down the same river, but while one has sailed along smoothly, something rocked the other's boat—some perfect storm of personality, circumstance, and genetics knocked him off course.

Letting Go of Hanging On

I must *Let Go,* even if I'm not ready—and even if I think my child might not be ready—because I can see that my *Hanging On* is weighing him down. Because of me, he's unable to rise to the occasion he so desperately needs to rise up to. If my child is going to find a way to survive his addiction, I must *Let Go of Hanging On* so he is free to soar.

My child owns his own life. I must *Let Go* of my belief that I can fix it for him or that I can do the work necessary in order for him to survive. I must *Let Go* of the drama and lies, the meddling and stalking, the fighting and the attempts at making things better (which only make things worse).

I must *Let Go* of The Addict (not my child) and all the things having to do with addiction; I must *Let Go of Hanging On.* And I must find a way to survive my child's addiction, while coming to terms with the fact that he may not.

Letting Go is a process. A slow and creaky process; the prying of sticky fingers off places where they don't belong. Letting Go takes real determination. And time.

Three Blind Mice

'Round and 'round we go, like three blind mice, running in circles around this thing that none of us wants to see. Bewildered and beleaguered, we don't want to talk about it either. Abused and confused by our son, our brother, who has turned into a loathsome stranger, we are a family that is wounded and hurting.

> *Three blind mice, three blind mice. See how they run, see how they run.*
>
> *They all ran after the farmer's wife, who cut off their tails with a carving knife,*
>
> *Did you ever see such a sight in your life, as three blind mice?*

'Round and 'round we go, in a spiraling plunge, from the happy family we once were into a disintegrating mess. A family beaten down with blame and resentments. A family collapsing under the wretched pain and destruction of addiction, which bears down on every waking moment. A family smothering under the weight of what it will never have. Of what the beloved son, the idolized brother, will never have. A family pretending things are still storybook perfect.

There's an enormous elephant in the middle of our family, but we don't want to see it. We are a family in need of healing, hoping for a fairytale ending.

*

Addiction is a family disease. One person may use, but the whole family suffers. — SHELLY LEWIS

Crummy Crumbs

Mother and child. A relationship so comfortably inter-twined until it's twisted by addiction. Starved for what should be—for the relationship I was promised before my son was even a bump on my belly—I've been scrambling for whatever attention he throws my way, no matter how nasty. I've been feeding on measly crumbs of hopes and dreams left behind.

But, just because I *want* this relationship to be more than it is doesn't mean I can *make* it be more than it is. Scrambling for scraps is not a relationship. I don't deserve to be treated badly by my son. I don't deserve the rude-ness and meanness. I don't deserve to be cowed by ugly scenes or slapped around by ugly words. I don't need a relationship so badly that I need to accept one in which there is no respect. So, I will set expectations and bound-aries, and if the bar is not met or the line is crossed, I will simply hang up or walk away. I will not allow my son to hurt me just to keep him happy—and just to keep him keeping me around.

It wasn't supposed to be this way. But I don't need to settle for crummy crumbs.

*

Love isn't a reason to tolerate disrespect. Neither is addic-tion. — ANONYMOUS

Be Safe, My Heart

The long, hard fight has left me scarred and scabbed, mangled by phantom gashes—and not-so-phantom pain. I no longer have what it takes to tussle the hustle. Sometimes, just when I think I'm on the mend, my next breath or next laugh turns into an unexpected sob— sort of like skipping down the road and tripping over a bump—and then, stunned and wounded, I wonder where it popped up from.

Be safe, my heart.

My addict has hurt me—stabbed me right in my heart-ache—over and over again. He has abused my love for him, and used me like a pawn in some unknown game. My own child has made me feel foolish and unloved. The pain of this has settled in to form a protective barrier somewhere deep inside me—one that is difficult to describe. Coldness? Hardening? I don't know. Distance, maybe? That can't be right since my thoughts and feelings about my son are always just under the surface— except when they're right out on top.

Be safe, my heart.

*

Give. But don't allow yourself to be used. Love. But don't allow your heart to be abused. Trust. But don't be naive. Listen. But don't lose your own voice. — ANONYMOUS

Easier Said Than Done

Yes, it *is* easier said than done. It *is* easier to say "don't en-able" than it is to actually stop enabling. It *is* easier to say "let go" and "love the addict" than it is to follow through. It *is* easier to give lip service to these things than it is to actually dig deep and do the gut-busting work required to have any hope of results.

Everything is easier said than done. But *nothing* is too hard if it *must be done*. And I *must* do my part in help-ing to protect my child from The Addict who's trying to kill him—so I'm not going to sabotage my success and his well-being with negative thoughts and words.

It's a given; everything is harder to *do* than it is to *say*. "Easier said than done" are words that don't even need to be spoken. They slam the door on forward motion. They are wants and wishes without legs. Instead, my words will be "I can and I will."

I can and I will, because I must.

Nothing is intolerable that is necessary. — JEREMY TAYLOR

Thin Ice

I tried to help my son by softening the edges of his very hard life. I gave him a safe place to sleep, with a pillow under his head, clean clothes on his back. I gave him money for food or rent and did all the warm-fuzzy things moms do to help a child when times are rough. I gave my son a comfy cushion, but The Addict took advantage of that.

I tried to help my son when it seemed he had hit bottom. I tried keeping him from hitting bottom by bringing the bottom up to him in order to lessen his fall. I wished for him to finally hit a bottom that would bounce him back into my life, but my son's seemingly bottomless rock bottom seems to be out of my control—no matter how much I wish this weren't so.

I tried to encourage my son when he struggled with rehab. I visited him when he landed in jail, and I held his hand when he lay at death's door. From my perspective, he has been at the very bottom of bottom. But the pain, the badness, and the miserable madness haven't been so unpleasant yet that my son is ready to make it all stop.

There's no telling when, or if, or how, an addict will hit "bottom." But "bottom" is not going to be hit while lying on a freshly made bed of roses. It'll happen while skating around on thin ice.

Just a Boy

It's all a matter of perspective. What we see in this world depends on our angle and is colored by what we have seen before. I used to "see" a selfish, lazy bum when looking at an addict sprawled out under a bridge, but that addict has been my sweet child, so I look at the fellow under the bridge very differently now, with a very different set of eyes.

A teacher, a police officer, a judge, a doctor, or a neighbor might look at my child and see a criminal, a junkie, a loser, a derelict, a troublemaker, or a waste of air.

But I see just a boy.

As mothers, we can help the people around us to see beyond the faces that cross their paths—beyond the stereotypes. We can help them to see *somebody's child, mother, father, sister,* or *brother;* we can help them to think about the tragedy of addiction. The people around us have only their own perspective from which to see things. By using the power of our voices, we can help them to see what we see.

Instead of a criminal or a drug addict, I was looking at a boy—just a boy. — SHANNON A. THOMPSON

Acceptance

Begrudging acceptance: This is where I am now. It took a long time to get here; I really fought it. How could I possibly *accept* this horrendous thing that has obliterated my child and my life? How could I *accept* that my child is an addict? How could I *accept* the fact that I no longer even know how to be my child's mom? The family is broken, the dream is dead, my son is suffering, and I can't help him. I'm suffering and no one can help me. There have been too many tragedies to *accept* any part of this. Too much agony. Too much unfairness. Too much wrong. *Accept?* Resign myself? Give the stamp of approval? Put out a welcome mat? I think not.

But *acceptance* of my son's addiction doesn't mean any of those things. It doesn't mean I am emotionally rolling over, giving consent, or submitting to the beast. Acceptance means that I *recognize the truth*. And I do— but I don't like it. Maybe someday I'll get to *full-fledged acceptance*. But for now, I'm at begrudging acceptance: *It is what it is.* Addiction has changed things from the way they were meant to be.

Understanding is the first step to acceptance, and only with acceptance can there be recovery. — J. K. ROWLING

No Shame in Being Honest

Not everyone is comfortable with my talking about addiction. I see how some people shuffle off as quickly as they can; others change the subject; some look at me as though I've sprouted horns. Some people say addiction is a private matter that shouldn't be discussed, but from what I've seen, there's not much about addiction that is actually private (except our pretending that it is).

I am going to tell my story. There is no shame in being honest. I don't want to pull everyone down a dark hole; I can shine light on this disease without doing that.

Some people think I'm brave for speaking up, but I don't feel brave at all. Addiction is a disease, not something disgraceful or shameful; it has nothing to do with moral failure on my son's part or my failure as a mother. So, it isn't brave at all to talk about my son's addiction, any more than it would be brave to talk about my son having a cold.

I have nothing to be ashamed about in talking about addiction and what it has done to me and my family—but if anyone is critical of me, *they do*.

Don't be ashamed of your story. It will inspire others.

— ANONYMOUS

Never to Be Wasted

Some people think that reviving an addict from an overdose is a waste of effort—they think addicts are bad people who will just overdose again anyway. "Just let the scumbags die."

Do we let the guy with a weak heart or clogged arteries who eats one too many donuts die of a heart attack? Do we blame him, judge him? Do we say he's not worth the effort? Not worth saving? Do we say, "He'll just have another one" (another donut *and* another heart attack), and let the guy die?

Addiction. I don't need to like it. Or accept it. I don't even have to understand it. But as a part of the human race, I *do* need to respect life. And, if I'm not going to make the effort to learn the realities of addiction, then I need to step back and out of the way. I will be quiet and let the people who both understand addiction and practice the concept of *love thy neighbor* take over.

Life is precious. Never to be wasted.

Our prime purpose in this life is to help others. And if you can't help them, at least don't hurt them. — DALAI LAMA XIV

Should'ves and Could'ves

When I look back over the years, time steeped in mirage and camouflage, I wonder about so many things. Little things that might actually have been big things, and big things that might have been red herrings. For far too long, The Addict was running the show, right under my nose, and I missed too much of what I should've, could've seen. I have no excuse. I have no reason. I have no clue. I have only regrets. But I cannot let those regrets consume me. It does no good to go combing through the past as though looking for nits. The could'ves and should'ves, the whys and what-ifs, are yet another train wreck ahead if I don't get them off the track.

When I look back at all the incomprehensible inconsistencies, there was (and still is) so much that didn't make sense. But The Addict was casting confusing illusions because he had something vitally important to protect. I must unload my teetering pile of guilt and mistakes before it tips.

Quit collecting every painful word, memory, and mistake. Collect hope. — BRYANT MCGILL

Ready or Not

I've waited a long time for my child to embrace recovery. I'm *still* waiting. I have no way of knowing what will happen next, but whatever it may be, I need to be prepared. He may find the recovery I've been waiting for—he may find a new beginning that will let us all live happily ever after. Or, he may recover and relapse and recover and relapse, bouncing along the bumpy road of addiction forever, withering away in a homeless shelter, comforted by whatever is in a brown paper bag. He may contract pancreatitis, hepatitis, or HIV. He may accidentally kill someone in a car accident and end up spending his life behind bars. He may overdose or fall from a balcony or find some other horrible way to die; my son played the lottery of youthful recklessness, and he may face the ultimate loss. I can't even think of all the possible eventualities, and I don't want to dwell on them, but I need to be prepared for whatever might be coming—good, bad, or somewhere in between.

As the saying goes, "Ready or not, here I come."

Be open to what you are least prepared for. — ANONYMOUS

Passing of the Baton

Another girlfriend is ready to pass the baton. Ready to give back what she cannot fix: my son. I've heard the same thing from so many girlfriends over the years; I think it must be a universal consequence of addiction.

So, I send off another reply, another *I'm not taking him back:*

> *It's hard coming to the realization that you can't fix the person you love. That love, alone, isn't enough. But after so many years, I'm excruciatingly aware that nothing real will happen until my son wants to give up all substances, forever. He needs to dive headlong into recovery as though his life depends on it, which, of course, it does. He needs to want recovery for himself—even more than the people who love him want it for him. My son is a wonderful person; I love him and miss him, and I pray every day for him to embrace recovery and come back into my life. I wish I could do more, but that's all that's left. He knows that I am waiting for him with open arms once he does that. Take him to the emergency room; the people there can help him. If he's ready, my son knows what he needs to do. You can't fix him. You can only love him as he fixes himself. Find peace.*

*

Codependency is driven by the agreement that I will work harder on your problem and your life than you do. This is not love. — DANNY SILK

Hope

I have a rocky relationship with *hope*. I've had high hopes, glimmers of hope, not a hope in hell, and I've had my hopes dashed. I've hoped against hope, pinned my hopes on a hope that springs eternal. I hope I'm doing things kind of right.

I always have hope that my son will really, truly get and stay sober, but addiction has taken its toll on my hope, so hope hurts. My dreams, reality, relationships, bonds, hopes, and expectations—they've all been pulled out from under me, like a rug. Tug, tug, tug. So I'm left without much of a foundation for my hope to stand on. *I hate hope.* (But even so, I keep a kernel of hope hidden away, set aside somewhere, for someday, although it hurts too much for me to give it a look.)

Tomorrow, however, is rooted in a tenacious hope. After all—after everything—I *don't* know the place where hopes go to die. Because my child is still alive. My love and hope have been thrown out there for my son to catch, and as long as he is breathing, there is hope he will come boomeranging back to me.

＊

While there's life, there's hope. — MARCUS TULLIUS CICERO

PART THREE
Wilt (a Bit)

Dandelion Wishes

I ache for my child to believe in what can't be seen—the relationship we had. The bond that was planted. I wish he could feel the warmth that once was there and push addiction aside. I wish he would reach inside and find what bloomed for years, until its growth became stunted: a child's love for his mother. But instead, it's a love gone to seed; like a dandelion after shedding its golden crown, all that's left are the tufted wishes. Wishes that will scatter on the wind of just one ragged breath. Wishes I'm wishing will drift their way back.

> *Mom, I don't really hate you, even though I've said I do a hundred times. What I hate is what I'm doing to you. What I've done to myself. To us. I push you away, not out of hatefulness, but because I don't want to hurt you anymore; I don't want you to have to watch me hurt myself. I think of you all the time, but I try not to. I'm so sad, so sorry, for what has happened. I love you, Mom. Hold on to that. Until, someday, I find my way back.*

My dandelion wishes.

*

Your mind is a garden, your thoughts are the seeds. You can grow flowers or you can grow weeds. Make your decision wisely. — RITU GHATOUREY

Sometimes I Feel So Alone

My son is a stranger to me. And it seems he is now invisible, but my heart still holds his place. Rarely does anyone mention his name. After all the trouble and trauma, no one knows what to say anymore; no one wants to ask when I last saw him or spoke to him or if he's still alive. Family and friends want me to be okay, so I act strong for their sake (and mine). But I hurt. Time doesn't heal all wounds—at least not yet. Sometimes I feel so alone.

My child is an addict, relegating me to a shamed and lonely place. The world around me can't comprehend drunken car accidents and overdoses. It doesn't understand addiction and assumes that this mother's love must have gone very, very wrong. Sometimes I feel so alone.

My child is in the grips of a scary disease, a disease burdened with stigma and blame. I'm afraid for my son. He is sick, maybe dying, yet I can't hold his hand. Sometimes I'm not as strong as I look. Ask how I'm doing and sometimes I won't feel so alone.

I tell you I'm okay because I know that's what you want to hear. — ANONYMOUS

A Love Letter

I wish you could see your life through my eyes. I wish you could see the love that has been following you every step of the way, every minute of every day. I know by now, of course, that my words don't have the power to change things, but I still believe in the power of love. I miss you, my child. I want you back.

I saw a movie recently about a mother waiting for word on her son who was being held in a detention center for undocumented immigrants. An undocumented immigrant herself, she was unable to go into the detention center to see him, so she would sit in a coffee shop nearby. When someone told her that she should go home, that there was nothing she could do to help her son by staying, she said that she would not be anywhere else; her son was in trouble and she would be near.

I'm sitting in the coffee shop, my child. I'm nearby, even if you can't see me. Me and my love. Love is all I have left to give you.

In French, "Tu me manques" means "You are missing from me." — ANONYMOUS

Love Is Pretty Quiet

One hug, once a year. That's all that's left of my relation-ship with my child (for now). But it's a powerful thing, this hug. It carries a quiet message.

Once a year, I make my annual trip, hoping to see my son. Hoping to reach around The Addict and touch him. Hoping to let him know that I will be there, full of love and open arms, every year, no matter what. Hoping to let The Addict know that I still want my child back.

We talk over lunch about my goings-on, and the weather—I no longer give motherly advice or lectures. I don't ask questions about drug or alcohol use, the things I can do nothing about. This is how our mother-child-addict relationship has evolved. We sip slowly on our sodas, but I know from experience it's best to keep our rare visits brief; *brief* hurts less than *one sentence too long*. Every year, we enjoy the moment and make a new memory to hang on to. Until next time. (I hope there is a next time.)

Every year, I just show up.

Love is pretty quiet.

I closed my mouth and spoke to you in a hundred silent ways. — RUMI

Remember or Not

My child, you won't remember this night, but I will never forget.

I don't remember how many times I've had that thought—after each crisis, each near-death experience, each *bottom* that wasn't actually a *bottom*. But my child was under the influence or unconscious through the most unforgettable events in his life . . . so he doesn't remember.

Oh, my child, if only you could walk on the path I've been walking as I walk after you. Then you would remember this night. You would never forget.

I remember too much.

And yet, I don't remember enough. I don't remember much of the goodness before all the badness—it seems to have been blotted out by the blight. Old memories, good memories, have been drawn away, like an old film winding back into the reel, leaving only the faintest sepia images on the backs of my eyes. But hopefully my son's memories haven't faded—hopefully he still has the re-runs to play in his head. Hopefully he can remember all the love, happiness, fun, and dreams we once had.

My child, you must remember. You must never forget.

✳

While the alcoholic lies passed out, anesthetized, the family goes through the years of his drinking—stark, raving sober.

— TOBY RICE DREWS

In Gaining an Addict

In gaining an addict, I've lost my child. *I've lost my child.* Nothing remains of the boy I once knew. The Addict has consumed every last shred. Not one piece of my child remains in my life.

The pockets of my mind where tender old memories should be nestled in, all safe and sound, are scorched instead. The pictures of my son, which should have been there for me to look at forever, are gone. Scathing words and appalling behaviors have smoked him out. My *him* is gone.

There is not a single boundary that the creeping invasion of addiction won't cross. There is not one bit of my child that addiction has left alone, untouched and intact. Like a scavenger picking through a cobweb-filled attic, I find that all sentimental relics have turned to dust. In the midst of this ugly storm, I'm holding only wistful fragments from the time before.

Quietly, in my dreams, when The Addict is sleeping, I call out: *Come back, my child.* But am I blowing whispered secrets he can't possibly hear?

*

I am strong, but I am tired. — BRENDA JOYCE

Forever Didn't Last

A child has died. Not my child, but the child of a friend. Technically, he was no longer a child. But still, he was *her* child. She was supposed to have her child forever. Except forever didn't last. I didn't know this young man. My friend's child. I don't know if he liked basketball or on what day he was born. My arms don't cuddle the memory of his tiny heft and softness, as though years haven't flown by since his birth. I don't know the feel of his hand—if it was calloused or smooth—or the sound of his voice curled around the name *Mom*—like silk. Or wind. Or leather.

No, I don't know the *things*, the *essence*, the *him* that filled the space in his mother's universe like stars, filling and fitting like only he could. But I can imagine. I don't know what dreams her child had for today and tomorrow, or what dreams my friend kept polished for her child. I never looked through their window of hope to the future. But I feel the slam. I feel the crumbling. He *was*, now he *isn't*. His mother has to find a way to live with that. This mother is a puddle of tears.

✳

One boy. One thousand feelings. — ANONYMOUS

This Path

You, my son, don't know yet, the love a parent has for a child. I didn't know it, *couldn't* know it, until I had you; the bond—the magic—that makes you a part of me (and me a part of you), no matter the years or the miles, as you make your own life. Even though you don't feel it (and *won't* until you have a child of your own)—even though you don't *want* to feel it, even though you stormed away and out of my life—you pull me along behind you. No matter how far off in the distance you might wander. And even if you never look back.

This path you are on is dangerous, dark, and scary—and, therefore, so is my path. There have been so many fears and worries over too many years. So many hateful words and sneers, half-truths and lies. My spirit is still crumpled on the floor by the door, still wondering about you, my child. Are you hurt? Are you dead? Are you ever coming back?

My heart drags in your dust as you walk this path of a million tears.

No matter how much you have hurt me, I still pray for you every night. — ANONYMOUS

Our Souls Need to Touch

"Mom." Sometimes a whisper will wake me up late at night. *"Mom."* It sounds just like my son, in his no-longer-a-child voice. I can almost feel his breath as he leans in, speaking softly in my ear, but when I open my eyes, he's not really standing at my bedside. He is not there, like when he was little, needing help in the dark of night.

But the umbilical connection is forever. Maybe, wherever he is, my son is in trouble. Maybe he needs me or wants his mom's comfort, and maybe I'm feeling that need. I can only hope that he feels the love I send back along the same path.

Sometimes I still have dreams about the child I rarely see and hardly know at all. Some are fuzzily pleasant, while others are vivid nightmares. But, either way, we get to spend some rare and unexpected time together.

A hug. A laugh. A walk in the park. A whisper. *"Mom."*

Dreams. It's as if sometimes our souls still need to touch.

✳

A phantom umbilical connection, unaffected by the passage of years or a long stretch of miles, mysteriously wanders the invisible world, searching for tears and for fears and for when things are not quite right, and then relays that information back to home base.

Say Something

The silence is too loud. *Say something.* Please.

I don't understand why I haven't been able to help you, to touch something in you with my love—or why nothing I have said or done has been able to match the power of the demon that holds you so tight, swatting away any hand that attempts to reach you. I don't understand the pull of the demon that's been leading you away from the people, places, and things that should be meaningful to you—and through torments that you shouldn't want to bear.

There's such agony in not knowing if you're alive. Or safe. Or a little bit happy. In not knowing if you've forgotten that you are loved. There's such agony in the silence. The silence has dragged on for longer than my heart can bear. I don't want to give up on you, on believing in you, on believing you will find your way back. But sometimes I do. Sometimes I give up on us both.

Say something. Anything. One word on which to hang my hope that things will get better.

✳

Sometimes the silence gets so loud, the only thing left is to hope your heart is strong enough to beat it out.

— RACHEL WOLCHIN

Every Freckle

Who are you? Where are you? This is what I wonder when I look into your face. I don't know you, even though I know the placement of every one of your freckles, and the first word you ever said. I don't know you, even though you sort of look like my son. Even worse . . . I don't like you. Well, I don't like the addict you've become. But, I know *you*, my son, are in there somewhere, and I would like to have *you* back.

Who are you? *Where are you?* This is what I wonder when I look at my life. I don't see you, even though someone just your size is ripping my heart and spirit to shreds. The toxic corrosion of addiction has eliminated every trace of the person you could have—and should have—grown up to be. The *you* you were meant to be, before addiction carved you from your life. And mine. The *you* that is gone.

I am drowning. Drowning in my lonesome tears.

One of the hardest things you will ever have to do, my dear, is to grieve the loss of a person who is still alive. — ANONYMOUS

Memories

I miss the old days, my child. I thought you might, too. So, I collected photos of all the people and places you loved more than anything in the world—until you loved the things that feed your addiction even more.

I collected memories of softness and giggles. Fond memories, memories of the younger and happier you. The real you, the *you* that you were meant to be—the *you* I was meant to know. Happy memories, warm memories, I carefully placed them into an album, hoping my gift would touch something deep inside you. Hoping to pull you back. Back into your mama's arms, so I could hold you a little more.

The happy memories squeeze tears from my eyes—and from somewhere deep inside my stomach. Maybe they make you sad, too. Maybe that's why you didn't want them. Maybe that's why the only memories I have of you, of us, are old and dusty now, like the abandoned album in the back corner of my closet shelf.

Sometimes I just have to cry before I can take one more step forward.

Hold him a little longer, rock him a little more. Tell him another story (you've only told him four). Let him sleep on your shoulder, rejoice in his happy smile. He is only a little boy for such a little while. — ANONYMOUS

Inching Along

I try to appear as though everything is fine, but the truth is, I'm trying to hold everything together—me, my son, my family. My world is falling apart and I am full of tears. Backed-up tears. Tears puddled right up to the rim, ready to overflow at any, *at every,* moment. I try to contain the menacing flood. I try not to cry except when I'm alone and no one can see or hear me. So I cry while folding towels near the thrumming washing machine; or while watering the flowers in the garden, where a tear can look like a splattering from the hose; or in the car while rushing out on an errand I didn't really need to make.

I try to appear as though everything is fine—a caterpillar inching along through each and every day, seemingly aimed toward a life as a butterfly—but the truth is, I'm about to inch right off the edge of a cliff. I hope I won't have to pretend forever. I hope there is an end to this feeling of doom. I hope I can fix what is so broken inside of me.

Dear pillow, sorry for all the tears. — ANONYMOUS

Nowhere

After all this time, I'm never sure who I'm looking at—my child or The Addict—or which one I'm believing (or not), or what to do or what to say so that I don't mess things up. After all this time, I will still pick up a nice sturdy broom and swoosh a pile of lies right under the rug.

After all this time, even though everything I've learned about addiction claws at my brain like fingernails on a chalkboard—screeching at me to *not* fix things, to *not* open an escape hatch, to *not* prolong and enable the devastation this disease still has in it to inflict—I will still open my mouth and butt in where I don't belong: in the life of my adult son.

After all this time, I'm still a beginner. I've been going through the motions—and am weary from the effort—but have gotten nowhere. Now, I need to set my beliefs and actions off in the same direction. I need to make my hard work matter.

I seem to have run in a great circle, and met myself again on the starting line. — JEANETTE WINTERSON

My Soul Screams

Babies scream and cry. It's nature's way of making sure things that need doing get done: a diaper change, a cuddle, some warm milk. Mom and Dad's instinct to *react* to the newborn's need for some sort of comfort seems to be delivered right along with the baby.

Parental instincts don't just dry up when the baby becomes a toddler or a teen. Or an addict. Parental instincts are for keeps. Even if they're just humming in the background, as things quiet down over the years.

But, what happens when every single nerve starts screaming at me to do something—and to *not* do something at the very same time? If my son were a different age, in different trouble, my instincts and I could rush to his side, without fear of contributing to his self-destruction. But with addiction, I can't be there for my child the way I once was. The way I should be. I don't even know how to be his mom. And so, my soul screams—which *feels* like a scream sounds.

Letting go is an excruciating heartbreak; mourning the death of what once was. — BRYANT MCGILL

117

Sands of Time

How could he forget all the time we spent together rocking back and forth as he nodded off to sleep? That time is as much a part of me as the arms that held him.

How could he forget the time we spent struggling over his math homework, or the time spent teaching him to drive? How could he forget the bedtime snuggles as we read books and talked and giggled? How could these moments, which are so momentous to me, be so momentously *nothing* to him?

How could he forget all the time we spent together on the floor playing with trucks, or the time we spent carving pumpkins, or fishing, camping, and hiking on our great adventures? How could he forget the times we ran around the house wearing capes fashioned from bath towels, or built pirate ships and forts from wooden posts and old sheets?

These moments are one big, inseparable part of the entirety of who I am. They are our sands of time. How could it not be the same for him?

✳

The worst feeling isn't being lonely, but being forgotten by someone you can't forget. — ANONYMOUS

A Soaking Rain

Let the feelings come. Let the floodgates open. Let it rain and don't worry about running for an umbrella. Wail and rant and yell at God. Fall to the floor in a puddle and let yourself grieve. Sometimes you can't hold the tears, or the pain, inside for one minute more or you'll burst. So relieve the pressure. Let all the things you've been shoving down inside come bubbling out.

Sometimes you just need to cry yourself dry. So do it. Go ahead and cry your eyes out. It may hurt, but it's healing. Let the teardrops fall where they may. A soaking rain, bringing new life to the wilted flowers in the garden.

Sometimes you have to let it all out so you can make it till tomorrow—sometimes you need a good cleansing cry. I don't know why it works, but it does. Once the storm is over, once the dark cloud has passed on by, for a little while anyway, your soul is filled with more strength than tears.

✳

Let your tears come. Let them water your soul.

— EILEEN MAYHEW

The Squeeze

I admit it. All along, I was winging it as a parent. I was always sort of hoping that some cosmic scale would balance out all the things I was doing wrong and right. I sort of figured that somehow, some way, enough of the things I did right would stick to my child so that when he finally flew the coop he would be able to handle the world on his own.

I never expected the launching to go without a hitch— I never thought it would be perfectly smooth or in a straight line. But never did I consider that it would be a total flop. Never did I consider that addiction would be the thing to muck everything up. I slog through each day knowing that instead of happy and safe and productive and surrounded by people who truly love him, my son is lurking around in dark shadows, living a wretched life full of pain and self-destruction.

My heart hurts for my child; it feels like a lemon being squeezed.

No one tells you that the hardest part of motherhood is when your kids grow up. — ANONYMOUS

Chafing at My Spirit

In scrabbling to unearth my child, so deeply buried under the rubble of addiction—in trying so hard to dredge up the treasure I know is still there, without any success—something inside me has become deeply wounded. If I could see inside where all this hurt is happening, I know it would look scraped, bloodied, and scarred. For as long as addiction holds my child by the throat, it will also be chafing away at my spirit; for as long as addiction controls my son, my wound will not heal.

Is my child sleeping under a bridge at night? On what does he rest his head? Is he cold? Hungry? Safe? Afraid? Does he hurt? Who are the people he hangs out with? Do people look down on him? Does he ever feel desperate and very, very sad?

For as long as addiction holds my child by the throat, it will also be chafing away at my spirit; for as long as addiction controls my son, my wound will not heal. No amount of time can pass that will lessen what I feel for my son and the pain he must be carrying.

It has been said, "Time heals all wounds." I do not agree. The wounds remain. In time the mind, protecting its sanity, covers them with scar tissue and the pain lessens. But it is never gone. — ROSE FITZGERALD KENNEDY

When Hope Hurts

Oh, there have been so many times I *wanted* to believe. There have been so many words that I've heard, things I've seen, and thoughts I've had that I so desperately wanted to believe in.

I so desperately wanted—*needed*—little sparks of hope. Little sparks that turned out to be duds. And so, there have been so many times I've been completely let down. *So* many times when I've had to swallow my hope.

"Hi Mom, I'm sober now." "Hi Mom, I didn't call on your birthday because I lost my phone." "Hi Mom, I didn't get kicked out of rehab because I broke the rules, but because the people there were jerks." And, "Hi Mom, I love you."—This may be the belief that has broken my heart the most, because it's often soon followed—in words or deeds—by "Mom, I hate you."

Hope hurts. So I just don't do it anymore. Except, every once in a while, I feel a little niggle of that unwanted stuff, so I guess I do have a little hope left in me after all.

False hope is sometimes much worse and sometimes much better than no hope. — MIKE CARO

Unrealized Dreams

Dreams. So lofty and pie in the sky. Like clouds. Yet solid enough to hang your hat on. So, for something that never actually happened, *unrealized* dreams are a heavy load. Like a dowager's hump, the weight has me emotionally stooped. The pain is crippling.

My dreams—for my children, for my family, for me—had no boundary. Some dreams were big and lofty, like happiness and personal successes, while other dreams were more low-key, like for everyone to be all snug-as-a-bug. I dreamed of togetherness at family trips, holidays, days at the beach, or celebrating life's great events—or being together for life's not-so-great events, too. Some dreams were as simple as chatty phone calls, sharing jokes, or checking in on what's up. My dreams had no boundary, and so there's no boundary to my agony now that those dreams are gone.

I mourn the dreams that aren't to be. I mourn the dreams that should have been, the dreams that could have been, and even the silly little daydreams and long-shot pipe dreams. Carried away, like a towering tree in a storm, things that once seemed solid, secure, and certain are gone.

Where do dreams go when they die?

✳

Nothing dies slower or more painfully than a dream.

— MELODY BEATTIE

Indelible Handprints

When I ripped the Band-Aid off your nine-year-old knee, it hurt me as much as it hurt you. When your heart was broken by a girl, *my* heart was broken too. When you weren't invited to a party, and when your best friend moved away, when your hard work wasn't rewarded, and when your dream didn't come true, I felt your hurt as if it were my own. Maybe even more.

When I saw the squalor in which you lived, the filthy mattress on the floor; when I heard that you were pistol-whipped and beaten and that you were shooting drugs into your arm; when I saw your puffy face and empty eyes—I felt your hurt as much as I would feel my own hurt. Maybe even more. You see, before I even knew you, during those nine months when you lived so close to my heart, you left indelible little handprints there. I was branded for life. Any time you hurt, the little handprints glow from their own heat. The mark you left behind ignites.

I've been surprised over and over by the power of this stuff of motherhood. It bloomed from some unknown place deep within me, literally overnight, and is virtually indestructible. But sometimes I don't want it, because it hurts too much.

Smothering

I never noticed before, my dark, gloomy spirit—and my need for lots of light and big windows on dark, gloomy days. This must be new; this must be because now *I am already being smothered.* When a cover of clouds rolls overhead, yet another layer under which I must try to breathe, the day-to-day clawing for air becomes a truly desperate scramble to survive. I struggle to put one foot in front of the other in the gloom of these oppressive days.

As the mother of an addict, some people might judge me as a failure. At times, I even judge *myself* as a failure. I often feel like everything I did, everything I tried so hard to do right, has been wrong. I feel like I ruined and wasted every single year since my son took his first breath of life. I don't know what I could have done differently or better. I did my best—and deep down, even on the worst of days, I know that. But still. The doubts and fears and mistakes are so very heavy. I must come out from under this weight. I must un-smother this mother.

Let it all go: the mistakes, failures, frustrations, tears, worries, doubts, heartaches, fears . . . and try again tomorrow. — ANONYMOUS

Dandelion Fluff

When he left, I didn't have gray hair yet. *Well, technically I still don't, but really I do.* When he left, I didn't have nearly as many wrinkles or pounds. And my nest is now empty. *It is a new nest, a nest he has never seen.* When he left, I had to figure out how to miss the child I love—the child who says he hates me—without withering up and dying.

Over time, I have weathered, in so many ways. Over time, I have fundamentally changed.

When he left, he was barely, legally, a man; he could reach back and still touch his childhood, where addiction began. Now, so many years later, he's stuck at the age it all started—the stunting of maturational growth is what addiction does. He has been living a rough life. A life that may have changed him forever, sober or not.

When he left, I hoped that he would come back. And, of course, I still do. But now I worry that I won't like the person he has become or that he won't like what has become of me.

When he left, we were still flowers. Maybe now we are weeds. Fluff on an old dandelion that might just blow away.

*

You may want something and fear it at the same time. You may find it both beautiful and ugly. — TRISTINE RAINER

Train Wreck

I have been out-maneuvered by The Addict, who keeps turning the *right thing* into the *wrong thing*. A train wreck (or two) is coming; I can feel it. A train wreck is coming if someone (or two) doesn't get onto the right track, fast.

I am hunkered down behind the protective wall I've erected in my heart and head, awaiting the disaster that seems impossible to avoid. I don't know the scope of the devastation looming ahead—I don't know when it will occur, or which one of us will be crushed first. Caught up in this slow-motion nightmare, I'm chugging along toward some unknown tragedy—maybe even my child's death—yet I can't think of what I need to do to stop it. I cower here, stunned into inaction by events that are too frequent, too awful, and too out of control. Caught up for too long in the tailwind of my child's wild ride with addiction, I have been dragged and battered and bruised. I wonder if I'll still be standing at the end of this ordeal, whenever that might be and wherever this might go.

✳

Sometimes we have to let go of what's killing us, even if it's killing us to let go. — ANONYMOUS

A Peek

If you could take a peek inside my head, my heart, my life, you would see craters and boulders and rubble. Unimaginable things. Insurmountable things. Broken things.

I'm talking to you, my child, and to everyone else who has not lived my life.

If you had a view from *in here*, looking out, you would see what addiction has thrown in my path—the things I can't un-see or un-hear, the thoughts I can't take back, the decisions I've had to make, and the promises I've had to break. You would see it all, without any nifty filters that make things look like things they are not.

If you could bear it in here long enough, you would become a mother who is fooled by an addict who looks like her child—one who still makes an appearance every once in a while just to keep things surreal.

If you spent some time in here, you would feel what I feel. Then you could try making it through a single day bearing my cracks on your heart.

I wish there were windows to my soul so that you could see some of my feelings. — ARTEMUS WARD

Today

Somewhere in the parental handbook, there's probably a small-print clause that explains my capacity to want to push my son over the edge of the earth *and* love him bigger than the moon—at the same time. I hope there's an explanation about this for him to read in the kid handbook, too.

I want my son to know that even when it might not look like I love him—and even when he feels like he doesn't deserve to be loved—I always do. But I can't just hope that he knows this; I need to *tell* him. I need to tell him over and over so that even through the days, weeks, months, or years that he and I don't speak, there's still such a big pile of love lying around him that he is left with no doubt.

I'd like to believe I will always have another day, another chance, another breath with which to say, "I love you." But tomorrow may never come. Especially with an addict. So, today I will let my son know I love him bigger than the moon—even if I feel like pushing him over the edge of the earth.

If I had one last breath left, I would use it to tell you how much I love you, because I do, and I always will.

— SANDI LYNN

PART FOUR
Feed and Nurture

Self-Care Is Not Selfish

There's truth to the old adage *If mama ain't happy ain't nobody happy*. But the one that says *You're only as happy as your unhappiest child* is false. The truth is *I can be as happy as I allow myself to be*. And so, I choose happiness.

Instead of smothering under my sadness—instead of succumbing to the omnipresent cloud of doom—I will fight back. I will do the things I need to do to *thrive*. I will seek peace, find beauty, and spread kindness. I will hang on to hope and healthy boundaries. I will forgive myself for what I didn't know before I knew it, and I will take comfort in knowing that I've tried my best. I will laugh and play without guilt.

I will nurture myself because I am worth it.

And so I can nurture all the people who love and need me.

Self-care is not selfish. Self-care is an *example*. An example for my children to see. Self-care is an act of love. For everyone.

✳

Perhaps we should love ourselves so fiercely that when others see us they know exactly how it should be done.

— RUDY FRANCISCO

Something Remaining

As my son grew from boy to man, child to addict, I had to let go of the things I could not change and the things that weren't mine to control—after trying for so long to change and control them. I had to let go before all the horrible words and deeds slithering in on the underbelly of addiction permanently destroyed the relationship we shared that had once been so good. I had to let go before I helped kill the child I was trying to save.

As my son grew from boy to man, child to addict, I had to let go of *hanging on*. Some things can never be forgotten. Some things can never be unsaid, unheard, unseen, undone. But, with time, some things become fuzzy around the edges. With time—left undisturbed, unprovoked, un-poked—healing can happen. I had to let go so there will be something remaining. Of *me*. Of *us*.

My love is all I have left to give my son. That, and something healthy to return to when he's ready. Instead of an obliterated, empty shell.

Raise your words, not your voice. It is rain that grows flowers, not thunder. — RUMI

No Baloney

I'm done listening to the nonsense and drivel, the hooey and piffle. I'm done allowing other people—whether they know me or not—to pull me down with their words. I'm done feeling incompetent or unworthy just because someone spouts off with biting criticism or smug judgments, catty comparisons, ignorant off-the-cuff comments, or insensitive slips of the tongue. I'm done listening to all this baloney, because, even though these people may seem superior from their high-and-mighty perch, they are not.

Words hurt, there's no doubt about it, especially when they're landing on already festering wounds that may never heal. But I will not let them stick. Someone else's careless words aren't what matter.

What matters is what I know to be true in my heart.

If people—family, friends, or strangers—can't be kind and careful with their words, if they can't pause and think before slinging fistfuls of hurt, I will let their words roll right off me or will walk away and let them bounce right off my back.

She made the brilliant decision not to let claptrap or hogwash dictate how she felt about herself. — QUEENISMS

Destiny's Ladder

What a gift it would be if, while I was working on being the best person I could be—the person I was meant to become when I was planted on this earth—you were working on the same thing. What a wonderful gift it would be, from me to you and you to me. I would know that you'll be okay, that you're doing the things you need to do to be happy and healthy, and you would know the same things about me. We could each live life to the fullest. I wouldn't have to worry about you, and you wouldn't have to worry about me.

What a gift it would be if we each grabbed the life we've been given—if we each climbed our own destiny's ladder—and worked hard on rising to the top. *You see, I can't climb yours for you, and you can't climb mine for me. One of us would be stuck at the bottom, having gotten nowhere at all, looking up with regret.*

What a gift it would be if, side by side, we could bask in the joy, the peace, the pride of watching each other—and our own selves—progress.

The greatest gift you can give somebody is your own personal development. I used to say, "If you will take care of me, I will take care of you." Now I say, "I will take care of me for you, if you will take care of you for me." — JIM ROHN

Gonna Go Get My Hug

Doors don't always have knobs and hinges, locks and keys, or little square windows. Open doors don't always swing wide in gentle breezes, and closed doors don't always slam shut with a loud bang. Some doors are nothing but figments of the imagination, and yet, at the same time, they are very, very real. I can *close the door* on a past experience, a thought, or a person with a flick of my brain—and it's pretty clear when someone or something is not welcome.

Some doors look like *arms*. Mom's arms. I could hold my arms tightly across my chest, or I could use my arms to push my son away, but I choose to keep them warmed up and open wide—a great big beckoning hug—a reflection to my son of my heart and my life. But maybe he's unable to see this great expanse of waiting and wishing and wanting. Maybe he doesn't know the door is always open here. Maybe he needs to *feel* my arms to understand this. So I'm gonna go give him my hug—and I'm gonna go get my hug too.

There are moments in life when you miss someone so much that you just want to pick them from your dreams and hug them for real. — ANONYMOUS

Let the Funshine In

I'm a naturally happy person with an unnaturally sad soul. My child's addiction turned me into this mucked-up mess. But if I'm to survive the years ahead, I'm going to have to straighten things out. This means that the two opposing parts of me are going to have to find a way to coexist. Well, actually, it means the sadness is going to have to take a backseat.

I'm going to find my old happiness in the midst of my sadness, which in no way means I've given up on my son. My sadness isn't going anywhere, probably ever, but I'm going to keep it tucked into a small chest pocket instead of wearing it like a hair shirt. I'm going to *live* my life.

I will watch funny movies and will laugh with my friends. I will revel in the beauty of colorful flowers. I will joyfully celebrate the things that deserve celebrating. I will sing happy songs. I will dance. I will let the funshine in. Without one smidgen of guilt.

Joy enters the room. It settles tentatively on the windowsill, waiting to see whether it will be welcome here.

— KIM CHERNIN

In My Pocket

When a mama kangaroo has a baby, a *joey,* she keeps it in her pouch, which opens at the top so the little guy won't fall out. There, he's kept safe, warm, and properly fed until he's fully developed and ready to hop away to face the world on his own. Once he finally wanders off, I'll bet her pouch feels empty. I'll bet she peeks inside once in a while, wistfully wondering how life is treating him now and if he's okay.

My baby has been grown and gone a long time now. Addiction has taken him far, far away. But still, I carry him close. Close to my heart. Close to the rhythmic beating of life's gentle drum. Steady. Constant. Maybe my son can't feel it, but I can. *Thump. Thump. Thump.* Knowing I'm keeping him close gets me through the day. And the week. And the month. I keep a little *joey* in my pocket; in my heart and in my head, I'm keeping my son safe and protected, and this is comforting to me.

*

i carry your heart with me (i carry it in my heart)

— E. E. CUMMINGS

Giving and Receiving

They say it's better to give than to receive. And that's true, to a point. But I think what they really mean is that it's better to give than to *take*, which is a more *grabby* sort of action. A completely different sort.

It feels wonderful to be the one who does the *giving*, the one to hand out gifts of help. But *receiving* is a gift too. For everyone involved. When I gracefully accept what someone else has to offer—be it help or a gift of any kind—*they* get to feel the wonderfulness of giving. The goal is for all the giving and receiving to flow freely and to naturally balance out.

Asking for—or accepting—help is not a sign of weakness—just as not asking for help isn't a badge-worthy sign of pride. Asking for—or accepting—help is a sign of empathy and trust, which is what a loving community is all about.

"I need your help."

Most people will leap into action upon hearing those words—moved from the bottom of their hearts.

She was always available to help others. Now it was time for her to discover how to let others help her. It was a gift that went both ways. — QUEENISMS

Peace

A duck in a pond appears to not have a care in the world, just swimmingly skimming along. But the fish can see what's up—the duck's little webbed feet are paddling like crazy to get her where she's going. That duck could be me. I am all calm and serene on the surface, but there's some frantic flapping going on underneath. I've been faking *finding peace.*

I suppose this is better than pacing around like a hyena or plopping down in a corner like a numbed-out sloth. But I need to find real peace. Down-to-the-core peace. Peace that will get me through the storms—like an egret gliding gracefully on the wind, no matter how turbulent the weather. Peace. Not *posed* peace. *Poised* peace. Peace that feeds my soul. Peace that has made peace with *whatever will be will be.*

Finding peace is a private process, but once found, it shines like the sun. Peace spreads warmth, which radiates more warmth; internal peace is actually very outgoing. So my mantra going forward will be: *Let the peace in my world begin with me.*

Peace. It does not mean to be in a place where there is no noise, trouble, or hard work. It means to be in the midst of those things and still be calm in your heart. — ANONYMOUS

Sculpted

I didn't know it back then, but really, before I had children, I was just a lump of clay. A happy lump. But still, just a lump. I was not at all formed.

Before I had children, my life was like *music* without having ever heard a symphony, or like *the color purple* without ever having seen its myriad shades tucked into a hyacinth bouquet. My life was lacking a richness and depth of which I was unaware I was even missing. But now, because of my children, my life is full and complex.

Little sculptors from birth, my children formed me into something better than I was before. With their personalities and problems, their smiles and their sass. The good, the bad, and the messy. I now possess a compassion, a strength, and a selflessness—and a whole gamut of feelings—that I would otherwise have never known.

Beautifully sculpted by my children—I'm a masterpiece. Still a bit lumpy, but that's okay. Now I'm complete. Now I'm *me*.

My boys have brought out the best in me and the worst in me—they've brought out all of me, and I'm more the person I was meant to be for having been their mom.

Handle with Care

My heart is fragile. My spirit is fragile. They're like threads of spun sugar; I need to handle them with care. I need to put soft gloves on the thoughts and feelings that might break me. I need to be gentle with myself.

All day, every day, I carry around sharp-edged emotions that are as much a part of me as the lines they have carved on my face. But every time such emotions give me a nudge, I don't need to respond by giving them a close look. And I don't need to grab them by fistfuls or armloads or boatloads, setting myself up to become overwhelmed. I can take out each thought and feeling, one by one, on an as-needed basis, give it the time and attention it needs, then put it back, very carefully, like a knife in a drawer.

I know the damage that can be done by feeling too fully the things that have hurt me. My heart is fragile. My spirit is fragile. I need to handle them gingerly, gently, softly.

Lightly, child, lightly. Learn to do everything lightly. Yes, feel lightly even though you're feeling deeply. — ALDOUS HUXLEY

Clean Sweep

Clean it up, clear it out. That's what I'm going to do. I'm going to sweep up all the old resentments and all the things that have made me feel wronged. I'm going to brush them aside without looking and toss them anywhere that falls outside of the inside of my head. I'm going to make a clean sweep with the broom of forgiveness so I am freshened and freed, not stuck in the same old mud.

The slaps-in-the-face and stabs-in-the-back came at the hand of someone who most likely did the deed and never looked back. So, by hanging on to anger and grudges, I'm poisoning only myself with a poison of my own making. *How stupid.*

While I'm at it, while I'm tidying things up, I'm going to forgive new wrongs as they come. Forgiveness doesn't mean I will *accept* new wrongs as they come; it means I will turn and walk away from kicks-in-the-teeth instead of carrying a vendetta in my soul. In embracing forgiveness, I'm no longer going to store toxins in my head and heart . . . or life. I'm booting them out.

Forgiveness doesn't excuse their behavior. Forgiveness prevents their behavior from destroying your heart.

— HEMANT SMARTY

Taking Care of Myself First

Whether I see a glass as *half empty* or *half full* depends on how I look at it. It depends on my outlook on life, which is colored by how I feel.

If I am worn down, emotionally or physically drained, everything in my world will be *half empty*. Including myself. Sputtering along on fumes that are clouding my vision is no way to view—or live—life.

I deserve better than that; everyone who counts on me deserves better than that, too. Me, my friends, and my family—we all deserve a *me* who's *all there*.

Whenever I'm on an airplane, I watch as a crew member spends a few minutes instructing the passengers on how to use the oxygen masks and how the caregivers in the crowd need to put their own masks on first, which makes sense. I'm not going to be much help to the kiddo sitting next to me if I'm keeled over, dead.

I need to remember this when I'm feeling depleted: *Taking care of myself first is neither selfish nor optional.*

You can't pour from an empty cup. Take care of yourself first. — ANONYMOUS

Perfectly Fine

After all this time, after all the practice I've had perfecting what should by now be perfected, I still don't do it—*anything*—perfectly right. I am a perfect example of imperfection, and I'm perfectly fine with that.

Perfection is an overrated and impossible goal—in fact, the act of chasing perfection makes *perfect* imperfect. Perfectionism sucks all the fun out of giving life a whirl.

Perfectionism is not a happy road to follow; it is harsh and demanding, full of judgment and fear. *Excellence* is my goal. I am on a journey, and I plan to enjoy myself, even laugh at myself—my quirks and silly habits, my screwups and flubs—along the way. Adaptable effort, patience, and reasonable expectations are my mainstays—self-acceptance and a love of this glorious mess that I am are key.

After all this time, after all the practice *you've* had perfecting what should by now be perfected, you still don't do it—anything—perfectly right either. *You*—my friends and family—are also perfect examples of imperfection, and I'm perfectly fine with the glorious messes that you are, too.

Embrace the glorious mess that you are.

— ELIZABETH GILBERT

Friendship Quilt

I have been wounded. Deeply. Heart and soul. Scratched and scraped, gashed and gouged. But, I'm still whole. The old wounds are healing. What's left is a patchwork of scars. Each one has a story—I know every horrid detail of every horrid scar. Like an old quilt, bits of yesterday stitched together one at a time, my scars tell the tale of a child's addiction on a mother's heart.

There was a time when my wounds were too raw for me to do anything but stay home and cry, nursing my wounds in isolation and hoping not to die. But I don't do that anymore—well, not as much. My wounds are healing—enough that I can move forward and help someone else. Which, in turn, helps me to heal some more.

I have been wounded. Deeply. Heart and soul. But in sharing my history with others, by exposing my patchwork of scars, by sharing familiar patterns and pasts, old wounds become a friendship quilt, warm and comforting, wrapped warmly around the stooped shoulders of someone else.

Healing doesn't mean the damage never existed. It means the damage no longer controls our lives. — AKSHAY DUBEY

Step Forward

One symptom of addiction is relapse. It is pretty common for addicts to be lured back to old ways—and the same thing applies to the people who love them. So, with addiction, there is always the possibility that today is going to be a rough day. Even with the best of intentions and best-laid plans, even when life's ducks seem to be lined up in a neat little row, someone or something goes and waddles off.

As far as moving forward goes, it doesn't really matter who slipped up. It doesn't matter who reverted to doing things they ought not to—*who* might have done some drugs, or *who* might have gone snooping around where she didn't belong. What's important is for everyone to get back on track. What's important is that we do not give up.

What's important is that I keep moving in the right direction, even on days when it's really tough. I can do this. Step by step by step. Tomorrow, next week, next year—they're all going to be better if, today, I take the steps forward to meet them.

✳

Hey, Beautiful One. You knew today would be a little tricky. Hang tight, Love. You're walking in the right direction. Just keep walking. — ANONYMOUS

The Wind Beneath My (Own) Wings

My family and friends have helped so much in getting me through tough times. I couldn't have made it to today without them. But I've learned that there isn't always going to be somebody around when I need support; my main support network needs to be what goes on inside my own head. I need to be my own first line of defense. I need to rely on myself, not someone else, to hold myself up.

I need to trust in myself. I *can* trust in myself. I have shown myself over and over again that I can rise up to the lowest occasion. I can count on myself to do the right thing when the wrong thing hits the fan. I can emerge from the darkest of places—still somewhat put together—all in one piece.

When and if the world is pulled out from under me again, I won't fall flat on my face. My family and friends have helped me so much to find strength. I now have the belief in myself—the wind beneath my own wings— I need to soar.

A bird sitting on a tree is never afraid of the branch breaking, because its trust is not on the branch but on its own wings. Always believe in yourself. — ANONYMOUS

Because I'm Worth It

Loving an addict takes a toll, both physically and emotionally. Considering what I've been through, I think I should look a lot worse—worse than the current state of affairs, with all the sags and bags and pounds piled on. Considering everything I've experienced, I think I should look more like a twitching, lurching zombie, one that's drooling and unable to string together a couple of words. Yes, loving an addict takes a heavy toll, but I can take steps to minimize that.

Every day I will do something to pamper myself. It doesn't have to be a great big ordeal. Just something to energize me or lift my spirits—something to unleash some feel-good endorphins. I will go for a brisk walk outside, but stop to smell the roses and commune with nature. I will primp in front of the mirror, and I will put on an outfit that makes me feel snazzy. I will make the time to do the things that used to make me feel good about myself before they started to feel like too much work and a waste of time. I will give little gifts to myself. Because I'm worth it.

Thank goodness we don't look like what we've been through.

— ANONYMOUS

A Friendly Line

I'm a people pleaser. So many of us are. I am quick to *help out* and *sign up* and *be there* for everyone who needs me. Usually, I like to speak up and offer to do what I can. But sometimes I'm just not up to doing whatever it is, for whatever reason, and I've finally learned it's okay to keep my mouth shut. Not everyone is happy with this, but I can't please everyone, and I'm getting comfortable with that.

Only *I* am aware of the jumbo stack of things already piled on my plate. Only I know about the mile-high mountain smack-dab in the middle of my path that must be climbed. Only I can sense how much more I can take on without cracking (it's okay, everyone feels like this sometimes). Only I have the ability to avoid being buried alive under the weight of taking on just one more thing.

Sometimes I just can't give one more minute. Sometimes I just can't be the shoulder to cry on or the person to complete the team. Only I can say the words *no, but maybe next time.* Whatever it is, for whatever reason, it's okay to draw a friendly line in the sand.

Boundaries are part of self-care. They are healthy, normal, and necessary. — DOREEN VIRTUE

An Inside Job

Happiness is an inside job. It really is. Life throws every one of us some nasty curveballs, but we have control over how we respond to what's lobbed our way. Simplistic or trite as it may seem, every one of us really does possess the power to turn our own frowns upside down. It has taken me a long time to believe that.

My child's happiness is not my happiness. We are two separate human beings. My happiness doesn't depend on his happiness or on my trying to *make* him happy. My happiness is my own, and whether it flourishes or not depends on *me*. Recognizing this as true is not a sign of abandonment. It doesn't make me a traitor to my son or the maternal race. It's simply accepting what *is*.

I start each day ready to smile—after my first cup of coffee—because smiling feeds and nurtures me. One smile lightens my load, which brings out another smile that feeds my soul, which fills my day.

One day she remembered that the only person who could make her happy was herself. So she took back her power, reclaimed her place in the world, and shined like never before. — ANNA TAYLOR

Molehills

My life is made up of two piles: the stuff I have no control over and the stuff I do. My son's addiction landed in my lap unexpectedly—I now know true devastation, and I now know that it can fall from the sky at any time—so I will never again create bad stuff in my life with my very own hands.

I will not get caught up in minutiae, making things into problems that don't exist. I will not make mountains out of molehills. I know what real problems are, and I am not going to waste precious time and energy on frivolous frets.

Instead of fussing about insignificant little clumps of fuzz that no one can see, I think I will just give names to the dust bunnies living under my bed. I will no longer even notice if someone squeezes the toothpaste in the middle of the tube or doesn't line things up in the dishwasher just right. And if I'm stuck for an extra minute behind some slouch at the stoplight, I'm not going to ruin precious moments by being all upset.

I know true devastation, and I know that it can fall from the sky at any time—so I will never again fritter away the moments I have control over with things that don't matter.

You just have to learn not to care about the dust mites under the beds. — MARGARET MEAD

Kneel

We have a rocky relationship, God and I. Well, it's probably more accurate to say that it is *me* who has a rocky relationship with *Him*. The truth is, He's been pretty solid all along. I've been the one shaking things up.

I have yelled at God, sweet-talked God, and negotiated (and renegotiated) with God, again and again. I have given up on God, apologized to God, defended God, and even dissed Him a time or two when He's made me mad. But, just as with every other member of my family, I know He's there for me through thick and thin—especially through *thick*. I may not always like Him, but I love Him. And He's always got my back.

All this time, through all my tantrums, God has never once lost His patience with me. He's remained a quiet presence that I can count on. And boy, oh boy, do I need that. I understand that my prayers aren't like rubbing a magic lantern, with expectations that all my wishes will come true. Even better than that, God is always there for me to talk to—He's there to give me strength and peace, to get me through the hardest times—and He's in everything I do.

*

When life gives you more than you can stand . . . kneel.

— ANONYMOUS

Treasure the Treasures

There was a time when I had to put away all the photos of my son. I had to tuck them in a drawer, out of sight and out of mind. They taunted me with too many happy memories that made me too sad. They were a reminder that addiction had reduced my life with my son to something that fits in a frame. The empty space where he belonged poured into mine, filling it with loneliness. But, things have changed.

My son is back, displayed along with his brother on bookshelves and tabletops all over my house. The photos and the memories still bring a tear to my eye, but now I treasure the good times from before. They are gifts. I am blessed to have had so many years of such happiness, and not even addiction can take that away. It turns out that, after everything, I still have my son's smile, the sound of his voice, and even his sweaty-boy smell after a long, active day. Memories. Treasures. They are mine forever. Flower petals pressed in the pages of my mind.

God gave us our memories so that we might have roses in December. — JAMES M. BARRIE

Conscious of My Conscience

I know that I don't *know it all,* and I know I never will. So I will read books and attend support groups, and I will listen to the opinions and advice of people who've walked this hellish walk before me. But there is no single, guaranteed way that will work for everyone, every time, for anything on this journey. So the final voice I listen to will be the one coming from inside of me.

I will not be hasty. I will not act selfishly or blindly—I will give everything I've learned a careful look from all angles—and will try sifting out fear of change (and plain old *fear*) and guilt from the mix. And then, when I'm done, I will trust my instincts.

At the end of the day, only I live with myself and my actions—or my decisions not to act at all—and whatever then unfurls. My conscience must rule.

I know that I'm not always right, and I know what's right for me may be very wrong for someone else. So, just like me, the final voice *someone else* listens to should be their own.

Listen to the voice of your soul above all others.

— ANONYMOUS

Polish Up My Spirit

Today is the day for positive change. A new beginning. Within me. So I will gather my dreams and start doing the things that make me happy. I will polish up my spirit so that my life and I can shine.

Today is the day I'm going to make the time, *take the time,* to do what is good for me. I might go for a hike by the lake, stopping to smell the flowers and listen to the birds. Or I might sit outside with a cup of coffee to watch the sun and butterflies start their day. I might go for a run—or go for a nap. I might cook my favorite meal and set a pretty table, or read a good book and nibble from a box of chocolates. I might volunteer to help someone who needs helping. I might take up knitting. Or yoga. I might go to church. Or get together with friends. Or listen to music. Or just sit still and breathe.

Today is the day I'm going to make a list and start checking things off as I do them. Things that make me glad to be alive.

Whatever is good for the soul . . . do that. — ANONYMOUS

Nuts

I'm a little forgetful sometimes. A little scattered. A little nuts. There's the time I was rummaging through my purse with one hand, getting a little frantic because I couldn't find my phone, while telling my friend all about it—over the phone I was holding in my other hand. Or the time I looked all over the house for a certain pair of jeans to throw in the washing machine—only to discover that I was wearing them. Or all the times I have driven back home to see if I actually did close the garage door.

But, I do have a lot on my mind.

Sometimes I'm unable to cut through the fog. Sometimes I just can't think a big thought or concentrate enough to read a book. Or remember my friend's husband's name, or the name of the movie I saw yesterday (or even what it was about).

Sometimes I'm just not paying attention to what I'm doing while I'm doing it. *I do have a lot on my mind.*

But I'm going to laugh at those times when the real world gets a bit lost in the shuffle. I'm going to laugh at myself so I don't go completely nuts.

It was comforting to me when I read that squirrels forget where they hide about half their nuts. — RUTH CASEY

Friends

Not all friendships are forever. Not all friends are meant to be a part of my life till the end of time. They might come and go, or I might come and go, but my life is blessed for having had them in it. The space each friend has held is a gift uniquely their own.

Moved apart, grown apart, or torn apart by addiction, friendship can't be forced past its time. Sometimes friends are at a place in their own lives where they cannot take on any more pain, and so they avoid anyone whose life makes them sad. Sometimes friends are limited in their capacity to understand something as messy and ugly as addiction, and so they might be judgmental or critical or cold. And sometimes friends are misguided and so help the addict in ways that aren't really helpful. Whatever the reason for a friendship drift, it's okay to let go of what *is* and just hang on to what *was*—the memories. It's okay to surround myself with friends who truly support me. Those who *try* to understand, even when they really don't, are the ones who help me make it through the day. *Friends.*

Just hold my hand and be my friend. — ANONYMOUS

Blooms of Hope

Blooming in my garden are signs of good things to come—a little sprout here, a tiny bud there. Teeming with the activity of bees and butterflies, a quiet show of healthy growth. My son's recovery is like my garden, full of signs for me to see, if I look. It is here, in what I *see*, that I can know what is really happening and where *true* blooms of hope can grow.

Deep down I have a secret wish; it's something I would someday like to hear.

> *"Mom, I'm working on my recovery. Sometimes I slip up; I don't want to make promises I can't keep, and I don't want to hurt you by dragging you along on an unpredictable roller coaster. I don't want to hurt you by faking what isn't true and by telling you lies. I can do this—I can and will find recovery. And, when I do, you will see it, Mom. You will feel it. I won't even need to say it—you won't need to wonder if your biggest wish has come true. Mom, I love you. And I know you love me."*

Where flowers bloom so does hope. — LADY BIRD JOHNSON

PART FIVE

Bloom

I Have the Power

I have the power. The power to change the way I react to the disease of addiction. The power to stop its destructive spread.

For too many years I was consumed by the poison my child was consuming. I snarled and yelled and argued and begged and cried; I renegotiated the non-negotiable; I rationally discussed the irrational. At night I either paced the house—holding vigil for his life—or dreamed of growing octopus arms to squeeze the life out of all his problems. There was no room in my head for anyone else; that's just what happens once The Addict starts wearing a beloved child's face.

My child was the one consuming the poison, but the poison that was seeping into our household was passing directly through me, sneaking in on the umbilical connection. I was the carrier—the Typhoid Mary of addiction—spreading misery and destruction through my family. Helping the disease to do what it does best.

You see, for too many years, I was trying to change something that wasn't mine to change: *my child.* The truth is, the only thing I can change or control is *me*—and that has real power.

Let today be the day you learn the grace of letting go and the power of moving on. — STEVE MARABOLI

I Will Honor My Child

Addiction is horrible enough without me making it worse, so I'm done with that. There will be no more ripping apart of hearts and lives—not by my actions (or my neglect). Not by my words, thrown around like poison darts. I will not blame or argue. I will not get sucked into dramas or force issues that don't belong to me. I will protect my boundaries, making room in my head for all the people I love. I will be calm, not crazed. I will be positive. I will have reasonable expectations. I will change the tune and change the dance; I will change my family's chance. This doesn't mean I don't care, don't hurt, or won't cry.

It just means I will fill the hole in my life where my child should be with goodness, not badness. Kindness, not madness.

I will honor my *child*—not the *addict*—with my words and my actions. The destructive spread of the disease of addiction stops with me.

✳

And that's when I became a warrior. — KAREN SALMANSOHN

Let Recovery Begin with Me

I can't make my son embrace recovery, but his addiction is not going to take me down, too—this will not be an airplane crash with no survivors. He will always be *my* child, but he is no longer *a* child. His choices, and his desire to make good choices, must come from *within*. I can't do anything about that. So I'm going to do what I can do about me.

This is not what I imagined recovery would look like—or who would be doing it—this is like looking into a not-so-fun-house mirror. But I will do whatever it takes to find strength and happiness. I will keep taking the steps necessary for positive change, even when it's hard. I will not be hobbled by thoughts of what *should have been* and what *could have been*. Instead, I will accept what *is*. I will accept the things I cannot change. I will find peace.

The hardest thing I've ever done is to acknowledge that I can't control my child's addiction or recovery—*but maybe the most important thing I've ever done is to let recovery begin with me.*

Life has ripped a great big chunk out of me, but I'm patching the hole.

Filling Not Stuffing

When my children were little, they hovered around the kitchen on Thanksgiving morning, eager to get started with stuffing the turkey. We tied on aprons, pushed step stools to the kitchen counter, and discussed who, exactly, would touch the pale and pimply flesh before popping the bird into the oven. Our home was full of pleasant aromas and things to be thankful for.

Everything changed once my son became an addict. Thanksgiving became a day stuffed with unspoken disappointment, anger, and fear as I waited for my son to show up—and as I sat down to a table across from his very empty place. Thankful I was not.

I've had time to adjust to Thanksgiving the *way it is,* to stop wishing for the *way it should be,* but time hasn't taken away the hurt—or filled the hole in my life where my child should be. I suspect it never will.

Instead, I've grown stronger. I'm facing the hurt rather than stuffing it away (usually), and filling the hole with things that make the day better, not worse. That means facing reality, not trying to re-create what can't be re-created, starting new traditions, and spending quality time with some happy old memories, family, and good friends. Things I am thankful for.

*

When life is sweet, say thank you and celebrate. And when life is bitter, say thank you and grow. — SHAUNA NIEQUIST

All I Want for Christmas

'Tis the season to be jolly, but while roasting chestnuts and jingling bells, I grieve for my child and his very tortured life. The joy of the season and the pain in my heart are like a tangle of tinsel or competing garlands of flashing lights. My child's stocking is no longer hung by the chimney with care, and none of the gaily wrapped presents tucked under the tree are for him. Long gone, even, are the days of robes, pj's, or other gifts that might be safe for an addict. Sadly, visions of sugarplums are no longer what dance in my child's head. He drags around his addiction like Marley's chains, but only he can turn things right.

On Christmas morning, my child will be far away—my heart cracks a bit just thinking of this. But I will spend the day with family and friends, eating too many cookies and making new memories. Gifts of time are the ones that really matter.

All I want for Christmas is my child back from The Addict who stole him, but that's not a gift I expect to find under the tree this year. Instead, I will wrap myself up in the peace of the season.

✳

I aspire to be a giver. A giver of love. A giver of good vibes. A giver of hope and strength. — ANONYMOUS

Like a Hug

I hold you tight, my child. Probably too tight, but I need the strength of my love to soak into your soul—and my arms must absorb the love I know you have for me.

I memorize this moment. It is something for me to hold on to forever.

I hold you tight, my child. Wrapping you in my arms, I still feel the power of our bond, even though it has grown a bit dusty from neglect. Our hug is a silent exchange of hope, strength, and eternalness, and a love that has been bruised but never broken. I kiss your cheek, leaving a lip-sticky mom mark, and now, again, I must let you go. I open my arms—empty but now full. Arms that will keep you snug and close to my heart, until next time. In letting go of you, my child, I'm holding on tightly to so much.

In letting go of you, I'm letting you know that I believe in you. Like a hug, I *let go* believing that you will find your way back.

✳

A mom's hug lasts long after she lets go. — ANONYMOUS

Seeds of Truth

I will be open about what addiction has done to my child and family. I will speak the truth with my head held high. Even among—*especially* among—people who look at me with disdain and discomfort. There's nothing shameful about addiction—the only shame is in allowing the disease to grow by hiding the truth in the darkness. Ignorance, ugly words, and harsh judgment end where education begins. So, as the mom of an addict, I must do my part in planting the seeds of truth and understanding.

I am not a bad mom; my son is not a bad person. Addiction is a disease that can happen to anyone who opens Pandora's box. I will honor my son by changing the way addiction is perceived.

Seeds are being planted. In some of the places those seeds land, they will actually grow. And, in time, they will spread more seeds. Truth. And enlightenment. Like fluffy tufts of dandelion caught on the wind.

I'm not afraid of my truth anymore, and I won't omit pieces of me to make you comfortable. — ALEX ELLE

United We Win

Addiction is a divisive disease, both in families and in public opinion. It pits everyone against everyone else, twisting and turning and confusing everyone into believing that the way everyone else is doing things is wrong.

Addiction creates a diversion. A free-for-all. A blame game that can't be won. The Addict does all of this on purpose, then smugly walks away from the hullabaloo, snickering about how easy it was to trick everyone into attacking each other. Addiction is a master at ensuring its own survival.

The truth is, we're all trying our best to make the worst-thing-to-ever-happen a little bit better, and the *only* enemy is the disease of addiction itself. Period. The path we walk is hard enough without adding the weight of judgment to someone else's load.

United we win; divided, addiction wins.

So, I will reach out with kindness. I will fill the lives of those touched by addiction with unconditional support, even when their way is different than my way. I will keep my eyes and heart and mind open.

It's one thing to feel that you are on the right path, but it's another to think that yours is the only path. — PAULO COELHO

Getting to Letting Go

I've had to figure out a different kind of *Letting Go* than the kind nature intended—I've had to figure out how to be a different kind of mom. I've had to figure out how to help my son without helping The Addict kill him, and how to make it until tomorrow knowing that my son may not. I've had to figure out how *to Let Go*, even when it seems harder than fighting the battles that addiction brings to life every day.

I've learned that I can love with both hands tied behind my back, and that I am strong enough to do the things I need to, no matter what. I've learned to only go forward, never backward. I've learned lessons that I can never forget.

While *Letting Go* might seem thoughtless, cruel, and cold to anyone who's never had to do it, there's nothing cold about it. Getting to *Letting Go* has been one long walk through the hottest fires of hell.

But, to *Let Go* is to love. I've learned I can do both and survive.

Dear Past, thanks for the lessons. Dear Future, I am ready.

— ANONYMOUS

Fences and Bridges

I have the choice to *not* engage when moments turn ugly. I have the choice to *not* allow bad moments to turn worse. I have the choice to say, without bark or snark: "I will talk to you later, when you are calm and sober." I have the choice to walk away.

I will aim for strong yet kind boundaries. Setting and maintaining boundaries with my child doesn't have to devolve into a tense, screaming mess. I will treat my child as I expect to be treated—with respect. I will pay attention to where I begin and my child ends, and I will stay on my side. I will only take care of the things that are mine to take care of, and I will not ask questions that are none of my business, digging for answers that I can do nothing about.

Fighting words, manipulative behaviors, resentments from the past—flung this way and that, from either my child's side or mine—are poison pellets that can't be un-swallowed. I will do my part in preserving what might lie ahead for our future. I will build my fences without burning my bridges.

A moment of patience in a moment of anger prevents a thousand moments of regret. — ALI IBN ABI TALIB

Fly

Back when my boys were little bundles of joy, I knew that someday I'd have to let them go. It was part of an unspoken, and unfathomable, bargain: I would get to know a love bigger than the moon, but, when the time came, I would need to let my boys go. When I nudged them from the nest, they would need to know I believed they could fly.

But addiction wreaked havoc on letting go.

I really only got to nudge one of my boys from the nest. The other left in a hurry, but he most certainly did not *fly*. With him, there was no easing of parental influence, the way it should be. A gradual process. The trading of an old way for a new way. A nice way for an even better way. A grownup way. Something more equal or balanced.

But, faltering or flying, both of my boys *knew how* to use their wings. And they still do. Knowing this helps make my empty nest feel a little less empty.

To hold on too tight and too long clips their wings and makes it hard for them to fly. To soar. Opening our hands, palms to the sky, releases them to be who they're created to be, not necessarily who we want them to be. — ROBIN DANCE

If Only

Oh, if only love were enough. If only love were enough to fix addiction. If it were, addiction wouldn't stand a chance.

I'll admit that at first I tried to sweep it under the rug. But just because I didn't want to see it didn't mean it wasn't happening, and so ignoring the problem didn't work. (No surprise there.) However, when I did finally face my child's addiction head-on, eyes wide open—all *ready-for-battle-bring-it-on*—that didn't work either. My love, my efforts, my wishes could not have been any stronger, bigger, better.

So what went wrong? It turns out only one person can make recovery happen, and that is the addict.

I cannot *love* my child better. All I can do is *love him as he gets himself better,* because getting better has to come from within him. I cannot *wish* addiction away. I cannot *ignore* it away. I cannot *love* it away. This is a hard truth to accept. But accept it, I must.

✳

When people are ready to change, they change. They never do it before then, and sometimes they die before they get around to it. You can't make them change if they don't want to—just like when they want to, you can't stop them.

— ANDY WARHOL

Nonetheless

The life I imagined—one big, happy family, both children (not just one) calling regularly and sharing news, all of us getting together for the holidays—isn't how things turned out. And none of it will be as I imagined, as long as *both* children (not just one) aren't flitting companionably in and out of my life.

The life I imagined was one for the storybooks, all pretty and perfect and overflowing with love. The life I *have* is just the opposite, but it, too, is a beautiful tale—in its own dark way. Although addiction has done its best to destroy life's most special bond with its hatefulness and horrors, it has failed. So, even though it might not seem like it, my story is a love story, nonetheless.

There have been times when I wondered about the strength of my love. When I feared that something might happen to break it. Or kill it. But the love I have for my son has been tested, and it is fierce. This is not the fairy-tale version of love of which mothers everywhere dream. *This* love is even stronger.

You have been assigned this mountain to show others it can be moved. — ANONYMOUS

Functional Dysfunction

Every family has messy stuff going on. Stuff they want to stuff into closets or under rugs. Stuff they don't want to see, much less admit. Every family has someone who's doing something that's embarrassing or illegal or immoral. Something shocking or scandalous. Yes, every family has a few skeletons rattling about, making unwelcome noise. But a little dysfunction here or there isn't what makes a family dysfunctional. A dysfunctional family is born when the family can't face the dysfunction head-on and still make the family work.

I guess addiction qualifies as *a little dysfunction* in my family. We've certainly, at times, disintegrated into a family that's far from healthy and functioning. We've been a family ripping apart at the seams. Coarse and crude and degrading, addiction has brought out the worst in all of us at times. There have been moments we've been the very definition of *dysfunctional family*. But now, we usually aren't. Functional dysfunction became possible when we shed the shame and disgrace. Functional dysfunction became possible with dignity, decency, and decorum.

Her life was not easy, but her fury contained enough finesse to walk through hell with grace. — JONNY OX

Bent, Not Broken

I'm still waiting for the other shoe to drop, the guillotine to fall, the hangman's floor to drop away. And I'm still not completely sure how I'll react when whatever happens next happens. But I'm stronger than I was when this whole thing started. So even if at first I swoon and sway, I'm pretty sure that, eventually, I will be able to stand up and walk away. You see, while my son's addiction has pummeled me—heart and soul and mind—day in, day out, for years, I am bent, not broken. Addiction hasn't won. Not with me.

I've learned to roll with the punches, to keep focused and balanced, and to be flexible when surprising or scary things happen—I don't snap; *I bend*. I've learned to face whatever happens head-on. To keep my chin up. And to keep trying to do the best I can.

Still, I have to keep myself in line. As with addicts, I need to work every day on my recovery. On keeping strong. And vibrant. A willow hanging tight in the mighty wind.

I assure you, I'm not put together at all. Nor am I broken. I'm recovering—finding the beautiful in the ugly and stitching it into my life. — RACHEL WOLCHIN

Stickle Burrs

The addict doesn't like to say he's sorry. He flings outrageous and hurtful things at me as he's plowing through my life, without looking back. So, if I were keeping track, there might be hundreds of things I should receive apologies for. Hundreds of hurts and slights and lies.

There would be a giant pile of stickle burrs stuck in my craw. Eating me up from the inside. There would be . . . *but there isn't.*

I want inner peace more than I want to live with inner turmoil that would mostly hurt only me. So, I've let it all go—the resentment and the expectations that used to roil my gut. I've burped it all up (oops, *sorry!*). The power to move forward, free from bitterness, is in my hands. It is not dependent on the whims of the addict.

I don't always like to say *I'm sorry* either. But I will. I will apologize freely when I make my own blunders, of which there are plenty, waving my olive branch like a white flag. I want to live without regret for words left unspoken.

Life becomes easier when you learn to accept an apology you never got. — ROBERT BRAULT

Flaw-some

I am so critical of myself. "My butt makes this pair of jeans look fat." "I'm too short." "I have no sense of direction, no idea which way to turn when someone tells me to go north or south." I'm constantly beating myself up. Big things, little things. Mostly inconsequential things. This has to stop.

I need to love and accept myself, flaws and all, just as everyone else loves me—and I love them. I need to love the whole package, not nitpick it apart into sad little shreds. I need to build myself up rather than cut myself down. I need to love myself for all the things I am instead of hating myself for all the things I'm not. I need to embrace the art of being *flaw-some*: knowing I'm flawed but totally awesome, regardless.

I am full of promise and potential, but that can't shine through with a bunch of negative thoughts clouding things up. *I* can't shine if I don't recognize all of the things that make me *me*—paying special attention to the things that are fantastically amazing—and keeping them polished.

Maybe this year, we ought to walk through the rooms of our lives, not looking for flaws, but looking for potential.

— ELLEN GOODMAN

Soft as Silk, Strong as Steel

I have a child who hates me. Who's slowly killing himself, and whose hand I've held as he lay dying. I've been afraid of this child of mine—you'll not read about that in any parenting handbook. His addiction has taken me into crowded courtrooms and noisy jails, smelly hospital rooms and hovels.

I've traipsed through it all in my pink lipstick and matching purse, hair-sprayed hair, and soft voice. But it turns out that this old gal is no shrinking violet. Just because I'm polite, quiet, and favor shades of rose doesn't mean I'm a wimp.

Be very afraid, Addiction.

I've seen and heard things no mother should ever see or hear. Felt and thought things no mother should feel or think. I know things about my child that make my blood run cold. I may still look like the cuddly old mom that I once was, but, while I'm soft like silk, I'm as strong as steel. I've been forged from the fire I thought would kill me.

Be very afraid, Addiction.

*

She may look like a fragile flower, but her stem is made of steel. — JONNY OX

Petrified Wood

I've heard people say—both addicts and their parents, once they made it through the hell of addiction—that they're grateful for the journey. That they're better people because of the fiery trail they were forced to walk.

I hope to be grateful, too, someday, but I'm definitely not grateful yet—*grateful* might be an overzealous aspiration for someone whose child is still caught in addiction's tight-fisted grip. Addiction has devastated me and my child—my whole family—and there's no end in sight. I am, however, a better person because of it.

I'm more compassionate now. More patient. More tolerant and empathetic. I'm less dramatic. Less judgmental. Less trivial. I've learned and grown in ways I never could have imagined—and didn't really want to imagine.

Through the unwinding of time and elements, I've been completely changed, through and through, like a piece of petrified wood—from sapling to stone. I can never change back to the person I was before all hell broke loose. But that's okay. I'm now solid and strong. I'm a weary, but wise, old relic.

Welcome the present moment as if you had invited it. It is all we ever have so we might as well work with it rather than struggling against it. We might as well make it our friend and teacher rather than our enemy. — PEMA CHÖDRÖN

Keeping Your Place Warm

Sweet child, keeping you warm has kept me busy for a big part of my life. Whether in the womb, in my arms, or in a soft, knitted cap I pulled down over your ears. Night after night I tucked you into bed, pulling a cozy blanket up to your chin so you'd stay snug-as-a-bug until morning. I warmed up the car for you midwinter and brought you warm soup when you were sick.

Like a mother hen keeping her chicks warm, this might just be a mother's signature move.

When I wasn't busy keeping you warm, I was busy worrying that you *weren't* warm. Like the times you headed off to school on cold January mornings, wearing sandals or without your wool sweater. Or like the times I feared you were passed out or homeless somewhere, without a roof, a bed, or a blanket, once The Addict was calling the shots.

I can no longer warm you with a scarf or some broth, but I've got you wrapped in the warmth of my love. I want you to know that I'm *keeping your place warm*—in my heart, in my home, in my life.

✳

I will never give up on you. I know you must walk your own path, in your own time, to seek recovery. So for now I will do the only thing I can: love you. — ANONYMOUS

I Spy

I spy, with my little eye, everything my child does. Well, I *did*. I don't anymore. But until I reined myself in, I snooped and stalked and scuttled about in every corner of my son's addicted life.

To keep on top of whatever was going down, I looked and I listened. I prodded and poked. I followed his tracks on foot, online, and in my car. I even had a small team of scouts ready and willing (and sometimes reluctant) to help me out. I was obsessed. And I was making myself sick.

I became a spy because I needed to *know*. Anything. Everything. If I knew what my son was up to—even though I couldn't let him know what *I* was up to—maybe I could help him out. Sleuthing gave me a convoluted way to stay connected to my son—a twisted connection seemed better than no connection at all. (Even though it had me by the throat.)

I no longer spy into even a single corner of my son's life. I don't snoop or stalk or scuttle about. Because knowing things that I could do nothing about didn't help him; it only hurt me.

Grant me the serenity to accept the one I cannot change, the courage to change the one I can, and the wisdom to know it's me. — ANONYMOUS

Lucky Stars

"At least he doesn't have cancer," someone once said, upon learning that my child suffers from addiction. I cringed at those words, stung by the hurt. I felt like the ongoing tragedy consuming both my child and my world had been entirely misunderstood and dismissed. And it *had*. But, still, that thoughtless statement gave me something to think about (many, many miles of distance later): even on my darkest day, there is someone else whose dark day is much darker.

Yes, addiction is devastating. My child endures unimaginable torture—day after week after month after year—and his torture is torture *to me*. Addiction is a hellish black hole swirling with hatefulness that keeps trying to suck me in. Very often, I'm so focused inward that it's hard to imagine anyone on the planet is suffering through anything worse. But I need to keep things in perspective.

All around me, people are carrying unseen, unbearable, unimaginable burdens. So, every day, I look outward, reach outward, with my heart. And I count my lucky stars, of which I still have many.

✳

I had the blues because I had no shoes, until upon the street, I met a man who had no feet. — DENIS WAITLEY

A Constellation

Our paths might otherwise have never crossed, and, if they had, we might have found nary a thing in common. Hailing from different states and countries, we hold different jobs and have different interests. We vary in age, race, financial means, and educational backgrounds, and we represent a whole spectrum of religious and political beliefs. In spite of these differences—differences that too often divide people up—we are the same where it counts, inside our hearts. Kindnesses, shooting out like beaming stars, join one another and another. And another. Understanding and comfort are shared with strangers who aren't really strangers. Tears and fears are eased with an outpouring of warmth and love, and hope is renewed with helpful hints and positive thoughts. Bound together by one of life's great equalizers, *we are the moms of addicts*. Differences be damned. Together we sparkle. Twinkle. Radiate light. A constellation of stars, together we shine in the darkness.

When you shine as bright as a star, two things happen: You attract other stars and you light the way for those in darkness. It's a win-win really. — IVA URSANO

The Same Moon

You, my child, are far, far away—I think you'd be far, far away even if you lived nearby.

We no longer share the same house or same dreams, holidays, or interests. We rarely even share a pleasant conversation. But that doesn't mean we're not connected. Whether you feel it or not, I'm with you every moment of every day. And wherever you are, we will always share the same moon.

When I miss you (which is always), and when I ache for some time with the son that addiction has stolen away, I step outside and sit down in the quiet night air, waiting for the moon to rise. I look up at this thing that is so far, far away—just like you are to me (and I am to you). But I know that you, too, can see it. Touch it with your eyes. And I feel your presence.

Tonight I will look up at the moon—the same moon hanging in the sky above you—and I will find peace in that connection. Maybe you will be looking up at the same time, at the same moon, too.

Our souls will always be connected under the same moonlight. — ANONYMOUS

Seriously

Seriously, I need to stop taking myself so seriously. Sure, coping with my child's addiction is serious business, but still, there's room for a giggle here and there. A chortle. Even a guffaw. I've been so laser-focused on trying to figure things out (and trying to get things right) that I haven't heard the cacophony of sheer ridiculousness swirling about—all the wacky things I've said and done, and that my son has said and done, too. Truly, we're more than a bit bonkers. But it's possible to find healing in the craziness of our antics if I step back and look at things in just the right light.

I've spent a lot of time taking the seriousness of things very seriously, but in that darkness I can also find light. It's okay to put on some gallows-humor-colored glasses and laugh at the preposterous things that weren't funny at all while they were happening. Other people might think I'm crazy, insensitive, or a tad morbid. But, seriously, I need a little hilarity in my life, so I don't care.

To be honest, I'm just winging it. Life, motherhood, my eye liner. Everything. — ANONYMOUS

The High Road

My life didn't go the way I thought it would. In fact, it went every way I thought it wouldn't. There was a time—and there are *still* times—when I felt sorry for myself. I would cry and complain about everything and to everyone around me.

Then one day, all pouty and puffy-eyed and peering over my pile of self-pity, I noticed the long stretch of miles left ahead of me. I still had a long walk to the end. It was going to be a miserable slog if I didn't come up with a better plan—one that was less sad and soggy.

So I climbed out of the place I'd made for myself down in the muck and moseyed on over to a better place. I stopped moaning and groaning, carping and whining. I stopped focusing on the bad and started looking for the good. I found myself surrounded by all the other people trying to stay on the high road—a happier, more positive course. I think this is what the Great Path Maker must hope for when he places such forks in my road—that I will choose the better path and live life all the way to the end in the way the gift of life was intended.

In this life we are all just walking up the mountain, and we can sing as we climb or we can complain about our sore feet. Whichever we choose, we still gotta do the hike. I decided a long time ago that singing made a lot more sense.

— ANONYMOUS

Pain into Purpose

I'm learning to live without my child, but, like someone whose leg has been amputated, through force of habit I often reach for the place he once was. The pain I feel is not phantom. If I'm to survive, the void left behind must be filled with some goodness.

There's so much hurt in the world—hurt is happening all around me, not only within me. There are other lost parents who are missing a lost child. And the children who are lost. There are lost souls who are hungry, lonely, or running on empty. I don't need to look very far to find ways to turn my pain into purpose. Ways to be constructive. Productive. Ways to help keep others from breaking, even as I mend my own self.

I can hold a hand, lend an ear, and watch over with care. For them. For me. But also, in honor of my child. Addiction has hacked my child from my life, but he will be with me every step of the way as I move forward.

My mission on earth is to recognize the void—inside and outside of me—and fill it. — RABBI MENAHEM

Figure-out-able

I was born—survival was my first success, right out the gate. I made it through grade school without falling off a bike or jungle gym and breaking my neck. I made it through the foolishness of middle school, the drama and heartbreaks of high school, the stress of college, and myriad jobs that were less than ideal. I survived the hunt for Mr. Right. And I gave birth to great big nine-pound babies—twice. I walked away from a rollover car accident with no lasting damage, other than scars on my head that look like stitching on a baseball. I survived all of this; then, I survived my children's efforts at surviving many of the same things.

Somehow, thus far, I've survived my son's ongoing struggle with addiction. I survived his suicide attempt and overdoses; I survived holding his limp hand for what I thought would be the last time. Somehow, I've survived the hatefulness of this disease that has stolen my child from himself and from me.

Everything along the way has been do-able. Figure-out-able. Endurable. I'm standing. And I will keep on standing. No matter what.

✳

On particularly rough days, when I'm sure I can't possibly endure, I like to remind myself that my track record for getting through bad days so far is 100%, and that's pretty good.

— VINNY GENOVESI

Carpe Diem

We rarely see one another anymore, my child and I. We rarely even talk or text. But on those occasions when the stars line up just right and we connect, I treat the moment as a treasure. I never know when—or if—this chance will pass my way again.

When we do have the opportunity to talk, we don't talk about his addiction. After so many years, there is no point—I know from experience it just turns into an argument about something I can do nothing about. Instead, the brief time we have together is for making new and pleasant memories to hold on to. Memories I scoop up in a tight embrace before gently tucking them away, alongside the old ones that are now faded and dusty.

The relationship I have with my son is not one that any mother would dream of, but given the circumstances, it's better than it might be. And I'm grateful for that. I will make the best of what little we've got.

Carpe diem. *Seize the day.* Seize every possible moment.

Enjoy the little things in life, for one day you will look back and realize they were the big things. — ROBERT BRAULT

Stronger and Wiser

I'm a whole lot stronger and wiser than I was when addiction first slithered its way into my world. I may have been a begrudging student, but I've learned a lot.

I know that I must take care of myself—I cannot win the battle if I'm losing my mind—and I know that self-care is not selfish. I know that the only person I have the power to change is *me*; I alone have power over my guilt and blame and anger—a simmering brew, which, if left untended, will result in spontaneous, destructive eruptions. I know that my love, like a bruised reed, will not break, and that it can withstand the most turbulent of storms. I know that I will do my best to do my best, and I know I will never give up.

I'm not ashamed to be the mom of an addict. And I will not live a life of whispers or slinking around in dark shadows. I've learned that I still have choices. And I choose to *live* life.

The women whom I love and admire for their strength and grace did not get that way because shit worked out. They got that way because shit went wrong, and they handled it. They handled it in a thousand different ways on a thousand different days, but they handled it. — ELIZABETH GILBERT

My Way

If my shoes are pinching my toes, no one else feels it, even if they're walking by my side and holding my hand. I'm the one who feels the pain in every step, so I'm the one who needs to figure out how to walk the path I've been set upon in a way that feels right *for me*.

I will talk about the disease of addiction, just as I would talk about any other disease that was killing my son, my family, and me. I need support and understanding. I'm afraid, and I don't want to walk this walk all alone.

Of course, The Addict would like me to remain silent; silence is what keeps the disease alive. But, just as I have no control over how my child manages his disease in his life, he has no control over how I cope with his disease in my life. I choose to live a life that is not full of secrets and shame. This is how I will survive. There is no one right way. But this is my way.

*

It's your road, and yours alone. Others may walk it with you, but no one can walk it for you. — RUMI

Strong Enough

Things might get worse before they get better. Or they might just get a whole lot worse. I have no way of knowing how things with my child's addiction will turn out. I have hopes for the best, but hopes are fluffy, like whipped icing on a cake. I need something more substantial, something strong and steady enough to carry me through if bad things keep happening, or if the worst thing imaginable happens. Which it might.

Fortunately, I already have something strong and steady enough to carry me through. I already have something so substantial that I can hold on to it and survive whatever happens next. I didn't even have to look very hard to find it. You see, I have my son's love. And he has mine. And, even if The Addict tries to fool him, I know that he knows he is loved now and forever.

Love. Love is the thing that is strong enough.

I stand in wonder at the wonder of this wonder.

*

Optimism is not knowing "things will be okay"—because they might not. Rather, it is knowing that you will be okay no matter what. — ANONYMOUS

Tip My Hat

There's a long line of worn and ragged people trudging down the road, slowly weaving their way in my direction, returning from the front lines. Stooped and weary, aged by the experience of years. They've *been there*. They've *seen things*. Shell-shocked and battle fatigued. I can see it in their eyes.

I stand in silent honor, not wanting to intrude on their thoughts, on their efforts to make it back home where it's safe. I'm hungry for their knowledge about addiction, to learn what they've learned about how to help, not hurt, my child. I'm hungry to know how to survive. Things I've not yet learned.

When the time is right, they will tell their tale—in little trickles or with floodgates open wide. They will share their war stories, their lessons, so that my own time in hell will be a little less prolonged. A little less harrowing. A little less hard. Their stories might shake my world, but they will also give me realistic expectations and fill me with hope. To those people who've walked this road before me, I give my respect and thanks. To them, I tip my hat.

To know the road ahead, ask those coming back.

— CHINESE PROVERB

The Same for You

Too often, it probably seemed like you were lost in the messy shuffle of your brother's dance with addiction, but, believe me, you weren't—at least, not in my heart. There's no question his disease changed the dynamics of our family, but this is just one more thing in the long list of things I cannot change. And I know *you* know I would've done everything the same way for you.

I wish I could make up for the times I was distracted or absent or crabby. I wish I could have given you a life that was more peaceful, quiet, and equal. You've never said so—you keep your feelings about this tucked away inside ten thousand boxes—but you must feel some resentment and anger. I wish I could fix that, but, just as with your brother, I know I can't and that your healing is up to you. In your own way. In your own time.

I am here to talk, to support, to aim you in the right direction if you ask. I will not harass and harangue. I do not want the toxicity of addiction to ruin what we have. All I can do is love you as you sort things out.

As a mother, my job is to take care of the possible and trust God with the impossible. — RUTH BELL GRAHAM

The Change I Wish to See

My son's addiction has left a gaping hole in my life. Falling in the hole or filling it up are my only options, so I'm taking steps to fill it. Steps. *Lots of them.* Nothing as difficult as the Twelve Steps my son will hopefully take one day, but if I expect him to do the hard work of embracing recovery, then I need to expect the same hard work from myself.

I will be an example of doing the right thing and sticking with it, no matter how hard. Of moving ahead, one determined day at a time. Of never giving up and never giving in. I will take steps toward letting go of the things that diminish *me.* My own bad habits. My own irrational rationalizations. I will take care of what *I* can, and should, even if my child doesn't take care of himself.

Recovery can happen even if it doesn't happen within the addict. And I've decided there's going to be some recovery from this disease. No matter what. I will live the example. I will be the change I wish to see.

So she packed up her potential and all that she had learned, grabbed a cute pair of shoes, and headed out to change a few things. — LEIGH STANDLEY

The Thankful Approach

My dad once told me that he thanked God every morning for all the good in his life rather than asking God for something more. Until I heard my dad's words, I'd been a greedy little asker, but I've found the thankful approach to be far more satisfying. There are no disappointments, and there's no better way to start the day than with a heart-load of gratitude, especially on a day that turns sour.

I don't always remember to start the day being thankful—especially when I'm busy rushing around for a strong cup of coffee, a hair dryer, and something that fits—but, when I do remember, it's possible I may glow until noon.

Positive thinking works so well for me in the morning, I've decided to start doing something similar each night before going to sleep. Once my head hits the pillow, I will start mining the day for something good on which to focus. It might be just the thing I need to fend off the midnight monsters that keep me awake. I'm going to think of one good thing from my day and hang on to it. Then I'm going to carry it into my dreams.

Grace is when we notice the near-misses we survived instead of the wishes that didn't come true. — NANCY HULL-MAST

Not a Game

One of the first things I learned as a young mom was that I needed to mean what I said. When I told one of my boys not to spit at his brother again or he'd be sent to his room, if he did, then *he was*. I learned very quickly not to ask my boys to do something ten times before losing my patience . . . and then exploding. Empty threats are full of trouble-yet-to-come. When I told one of my boys to be ready on time in the morning or he'd have to walk to school—because he was always making his brother late—and he wasn't on time the next day, *he walked*. (Once. It never happened again.) Life was much more pleasant when my children didn't need to navigate through my wishy-washiness.

Now that my kids are grown, when I set boundaries, I still need to follow through. Especially with The Addict. He will pounce at the slightest weakness, picking and prying for more cracks, manipulating me and playing me like a fool. But I will not engage.

My rules are still clear and predictable, but this is not a game.

*

The only way to win with a toxic person is not to play.

— ANONYMOUS

Someone Else

The eye roll. Every parent knows the meaning of *that*. Something we've said is really stupid. Or corny. Or embarrassing. And the eye-rolling child is aghast.

I've shared my best pearls of wisdom with my children, only to have them look at me as though I'm an ancient dinosaur with two heads. But when someone else repeats the same thing someday, my children are in awe and act as though they had never heard the words before, even though I'd repeated them a dozen times.

"Hey Mom, you were right. You're so smart," said no child, ever. And that's okay. Because my dusty old gems are stored away somewhere, making it easier for my children to hear the message when it's time. But sometimes I'm not the one who is supposed to bring home a particular message. Sometimes a message needs to be delivered by someone else. Sometimes it is someone else's voice that will resonate.

It may be someone else who will bring my addicted child home.

When your children are teenagers, it's important to have a dog so that someone in the house is happy to see you.

— NORA EPHRON

Better, Not Bitter

Life was so good before addiction wormed its way in. Pleasant patches of ordinariness sewn together with love . . . oh, how I long for those gloriously humdrum old days. But, I'm dealing with *what is,* instead of making dandelion wishes for things to be different.

Inspiration is sometimes rooted in suffering, and there's certainly been plenty of that, so I will use it to help others in this place where love and addiction meet. Trying to lead them out of the shadows, shining a light in dark corners, and showing them where to look for a recovery of their own.

Hurt people often hurt people—I don't want to do that. So I will take care not to criticize, judge, or ridicule. I will not be sucked into gossip and cruel chatter. I will be optimistic, not cynical. If it's not kind or helpful, I won't say it. If I can't leave the world and the people around me in a better place, I can, at least, not make it worse.

Life was so good before addiction wormed its way in. But I will find ways to make myself better, not bitter.

Be soft. Do not let the world make you hard. Do not let pain make you hate. Do not let the bitterness steal your sweetness. — IAIN S. THOMAS

Success

Just as I cannot take credit for my children's successes, neither can I bear the weight of their mistakes. My value isn't built upon what my boys do or don't do—it's built on my very own steps and actions. It's built on the smiles and warm words, the efforts I myself make, every day, to leave the world a better place. My value is my own—and biggest—success.

Some of my successes are more exciting than others. More grandiose. Like getting hired for a prized job or crossing the finish line in a long race. But some days it's a huge success just to get out of bed or brush my hair. I don't need to weigh my successes against each other—or anyone else's. I just need to recognize a success when it happens and give myself a pat on the back. There is great value in small successes: like steps on a ladder, they take me from the lowest point, and everywhere in between, all the way to the top.

Success is sometimes just having one more patch than you have holes in your inner tube. — LEIGH STANDLEY

His Worst Enemy

There was a time when I was tricked, manipulated, and hated into helping The Addict. Placating, fearful, even groveling, my love crouched behind a mirage of wishful thinking, lobbing out whatever it could to keep The Addict happy. I believed that I was making things better somehow if I gave him money, let him use the car, believed his lies, or smiled when he hurt me.

I so desperately wanted to demonstrate my love, even if my love was all twisted. But not anymore. My love has been straightened out.

My love is no longer confused by delusion. The Addict's hatred no longer has the power to get me all muddled up. Because it's not *The Addict* I hope will be grateful for my love. *It's my child. My child* is the one who needs my support. *My child* needs to see my strength. My devotion. My resolve.

My child needs me to face down his worst enemy, not help it.

My child is the one I want to see live beyond tomorrow.

"You've always had the power my dear, you just had to find it for yourself." — GLINDA THE GOOD WITCH, *THE WIZARD OF OZ*

Connect the Jots

When the child I once trusted started to lie and cheat and steal, I began to collect the confusing scraps swirling around me, inspecting each one carefully, and storing it right up front in my befuddled mind.

I needed to keep all the pieces fresh and handy in order to make sense of the next lie—to make sense of what was happening—which, of course, was an activity that made no sense at all. Day and night, I kept this morass of lies and fears churning—until I started to jot things down. Only then did I start to let go. Because, instead of wearing the noose that was killing me, I let it unravel behind my scribbled words.

My notebook was a place for me to dump all my troubles, a place for me to search if I needed clues or missing pieces to the latest puzzle, but writing was so much more than the freeing up of space in my spirit and mind. Writing allowed me to see what was so much more obvious on paper—*I was doing and saying and believing the same things over and over.* Writing allowed me to connect the jots: nothing is going to change unless *I* make the change. Change is up to *me*.

*

I gently fondle old memories—the fragile snowflakes of time—and put them in the safe and everlasting place of words, not to be altered or forgotten in the ravages of this ongoing storm.

The One Who Matters

Once I stopped caring if *The Addict* hated me, The Addict hated me even more. He didn't like the word *no*. He yelled and cursed and threatened, viciously pulling my heartstrings and feeding my fears, trying to trick me into betraying *my child*.

But I didn't.

My love is a rock-solid foundation for *my child*—not *The Addict*—to stand on, to take his next step.

My love for *my child* is unshakable, and now they both know it. I said it out loud. I said it through my actions. I made it really clear. Eventually The Addict's manipulative gyrations completely stopped, but that's not the end of the story. Sometimes, I'm still able to speak with my child, or he'll reach out to me to let me know he's still there.

> *"Hi Mom. I was thinking of you and just wanna say 'I love you.' I feel like I'm missing out on my amazing mom because I don't call very often. Hug toss."*

For many years now, the only thing I've been able to do for my child is love him. *Love him.* *The Addict* may hate me, but *my child* doesn't. And *my child* is the one who matters.

No one else will ever know the strength of my love for you. After all, you're the only one who knows what my heart sounds like from the inside. — KRISTEN PROBY

Mother's Day

It has been many years since *both* of my children remembered me on Mother's Day. I know it's just a manufactured holiday, but still, it hurts not being loved and appreciated on the "official day" of maternal love and appreciation. It hurts that The Addict has turned my son against me so much that he can't muster up enough fondness to even send a text.

But, Mother's Day isn't just about soaking up the love and appreciation of my children; it's just as much about reveling in the blessings of *being* a mother. The gifts. So I will focus on that. *I will always be a mother.* I was given two precious miracles, one to hold in each hand. Nothing can take away the splendor of that.

Perhaps the butterfly is proof that you can go through a great deal of darkness, yet become something beautiful.

— ANONYMOUS

No Longer a Doormat

Every time my child was convinced or cornered into going into treatment for his addiction, he played it—and me and everyone else around him—like a game and then walked away.

When my child was arrested—the times I knew about—I showed up in court as a reminder that he was loved and that he had reason to head in another direction; I even stayed when he bared his teeth at me and hissed. I wrote letters to the judge, doing damage control, pleading for my child to be sentenced to rehab not jail, and then listened as my child blamed everyone he could think of for why he did end up in jail—the only person not to blame was the one looking at me from the other side of the smudged glass.

I loaned my child money when times were tough, but not wanting to make times any tougher, I didn't ask him to pay the money back. I made excuses for his self-centered meanness and pretended not to hurt when he missed my birthday or when his place at our Thanksgiving table remained empty.

What I allow is what will continue. And *The Addict* will take advantage of that. But he's in for a surprise. I will no longer be his doormat.

*

If others know you have wishy-washy boundaries, then they are free to walk all over you; the result is that you become a doormat. — DAVID W. EARLE

Busybody Barrier

Learning to mind my own business is like rolling up a car window that's a little bit stuck; a busybody barrier, I can see what's going on, but (reluctantly at times) it keeps my nose from poking around where it doesn't belong. Learning to mind my own business is a healthy and respectful show of love, for everyone whose business I might be inclined to butt in on, and even for myself.

Minding my own business lets everyone know I believe they are capable of doing (or noticing) whatever it is that I think should be done (or noticed). It lets them know that my way is not the only way and that I'm not the only one who can do things right. Minding my own business means *waiting to be asked* and *keeping my mouth shut* and *not fixing things that aren't mine to fix*. It *doesn't* mean jumping into someone else's life with both feet and a bunch of opinions.

Learning to mind my own business is a slow and stubborn process. But it's like figuring out how *not* to be the *unwelcome guest*, so it's worth it.

As I recover, I am learning to detach with love and mind my own business with dignity. — KATHY KENDALL

Change the Dance

If my child—or anyone, for that matter—pulls me into a cussing-screaming match, I don't need to yell back even louder and stay engaged until the bitter end. I don't need to get caught up in the swirl of the whirling dervish dance, which will get me nowhere fast.

I can go another way, I can go somewhere else. I can calmly say, "I would love to talk about this, but not when you're yelling. When you're ready to talk to me without raising your voice, I will be in the other room." By leaving, without stomping off, I can let the getting-nowhere go. My child holds the dance card, and knows where to find me, if he still wants to dance.

If my child (or anyone, for that matter) pulls me into a battle of wills—if our horns are locked in a cloddish waltz—I can put a stop to the swirl of getting nowhere if I simply *stop pushing back*. Once my child has nothing to push against, once the battle against *me* is no longer the focus of his efforts, my child is freed up to focus on the issue at hand.

All I need to do is change the dance.

✳

People get locked into a rut of trying harder without trying smarter. Trying harder doesn't always work. Sometimes we need to do something radically different.

– CHICKEN SOUP FOR THE SOUL

Heart On and Hands Off

I made a lot of mistakes trying to help my son, sometimes treating him like a child even though he was an adult, and treating him like an adult when he was acting like a child. I tried soft love and tough love. I tried keeping him from hitting bottom, raising the bottom up for him, and getting him help when I thought he'd finally hit bottom (over and over again). I fumbled around with helping and enabling, trying so hard to stay on the right side of the invisible line between helping him to live and helping him to die. Through trial and error and lack of results, I learned that I can't fix my son's addiction for him. In fact, I learned that by keeping my hand in things, I was making things worse.

I wish I could make my child think and do the things he needs to think and do in order to embrace recovery and get himself better, but I can't. Only he can do that. He needs to be his own hero. But I can still be his biggest cheerleader. Heart on and hands off.

But above all, I wish for your happiness, even though I am aware you require my absence to find it. — BEAU TAPLIN

Enlightened Place in Time

Loving a child who suffers with addiction is a uniquely staggering grief. I've never felt so incapable and helpless, so sad, so lonely. Such fear. My child has been stolen from me—stolen from *himself*—and I mourn this tragedy from a very solitary place. But it's up to *me* to help the people who love me to help me—and to help them help me to help my beloved addict. It's up to *me* to enlighten them. It's up to *me* to ask for their efforts at understanding and support. It's too much to expect that all this will happen by itself.

I can talk and give them books and take them to meetings, but not everyone around me—even members of my own family—will be able (or willing) to see the truths of addiction. Not everyone will be able (or willing) to give me the comfort I need. No matter what I say or do, some people will stay stuck in the mud of their own judgment and ignorance. I need to accept this and move on; understanding and support cannot be crammed in where it doesn't fit. I need to walk away until they reach a more enlightened place in time.

For every ailment under the sun, there is a remedy, or there is none. If there be one, try to find it; if there is none, never mind it. — MOTHER GOOSE

I Think You Can, I Think You Can

Just as with every other disease, the diagnosis of addiction establishes responsibility and expectation, and a specific treatment plan must be followed. But, unlike any other disease, *this* diagnosis is too often looked upon as an *excuse*. Or gets all snarled up in a twist of guilt or manipulation.

Disease—all disease—is a sad, unfair, and unwelcome fact of life. Addiction is no different. My child needs to learn how to manage this disease in his life because he is the one *living his life*. No one can take his medicine for him. My child is not responsible for *having* this disease, but he *is* responsible for his own actions and behavior, and for the success of his own recovery. Any choices, decisions, rewards, results, and consequences are completely and totally his. He is the only person who can manage his disease and put together the pieces of his life.

My message to my child is loud and clear: "I love you. I believe in you. And *I think you can do this*."

As much as I wish otherwise, my child's journey is not my journey. I can't do this for him. He needs to learn how to *live* his life.

*

Help people help themselves. . . . Don't make your journey theirs, nor make their journey yours. — STEVE MARABOLI

A Reason to Change

There may be nothing I can say or do to stop my child from doing what he's doing—there may be nothing I can say or do to make him change. But he needs to have a *reason* to stop. A *reason* to change.

The pull of addiction needs to be counterbalanced by the obstinate presence of love. I will protect my boundaries—I will not allow myself to be drawn into the addict's destructive chaos—but as long as my child is alive, I will find ways to sprinkle my love right alongside of my *letting go*. I may be sitting on the sideline, but my child needs to know there's nobody rooting harder for him to make it back into the game. My words and my actions will be soft and reasonable, instead of angry bombs that will irreparably damage our future. My child needs to know that he is with me, forever and always.

There may be nothing I can say or do to stop my child from doing what he's doing—there may be nothing I can say or do to make him change. But he needs to have a *reason* to stop. A *reason* to change.

Love is the reason.

✳

No one can change a person, but a person can be the reason someone changes. — SHANNON L. ADLER

What Blooms

Some days, I become overwhelmed with the wrongness of everything. With not understanding what has happened. Or how or why. Some days, I allow myself to think of all the worst things that have happened and that might still happen. And I allow myself to think that things will never, ever get better. Some days, I just have to wallow around for a while.

Then, when I'm done being morose, I remember that things *will* never, ever get better if I don't help them along. I remember that *things getting better* grows from the inside out. What blooms is what was planted; my tomorrow starts with that.

Some days, I need to work extra hard on my inner serenity—knowing there's such healing power in that. I need to remind myself to keep my heart open to trust and hope and honesty. I remind myself that happy memories, peaceful memories, like flowers in a garden, are beautiful gifts. So I collect those memories and let them gently tickle my mind. And I remind myself to fill my thoughts, my world, with happy things, not sad things; *right* things, not *wrong* things.

Whatever is good. I remind myself, daily, to grow that.

✳

Pear seeds grow into pear trees, nut seeds into nut trees, and God-seed into God. — MEISTER ECKHART

PART SIX

Scatter Goodness

Pay It Sideways

Burdened with a hard-earned weight of understanding, I know that I can do nothing more to help my son. Not directly, anyway. I know this because I have lived and breathed *trying*. But I believe my love and hope for him can come full circle in unexpected ways. I can *pay it sideways*, letting my love and hope flow outward in ripples and waves.

Just as I am unable to help my child, other moms are out there who, for whatever reason, are unable to do their mom-stuff, too. And these moms probably feel every bit as helpless as I do. But, if I reach out to help someone, anyone, then someday, in some way, maybe I will help their child, and maybe someday, in some way, someone will help my child too. Maybe someday, someone will say or do some little thing that will make a difference when he hits a rough patch, setting his life on a better course.

Maybe someday, the ripple effect of kindness will reach the people we moms cannot. My child. And theirs.

*

It has been said something as small as the flutter of a butterfly's wing can ultimately cause a typhoon halfway around the world. — CHAOS THEORY

Three Things

It's true. What really matters *isn't* the size of my house, the model of my car, the size of my bank account, or whether I'm a celebrity or crowd pleaser. (*Admired,* I think, is a different beast because it means that someone is doing something right.)

What really matters *isn't* the fights I won, the points I scored, or how many times I was right or had the last word.

What really matters *isn't* the tally of my achievements or even the tally of all the people I love who love me back (although this is pretty nice, I can't control how other people feel about me, even if I'm being especially nice).

What really matters *is* how I treat other people. What really matters is that my actions are guided by good intentions and that my words are kind, necessary, and true. (These three things alone could change the world.)

I won't know when I'm beginning the end of my story, so I'm going to be sure to make every moment a moment to be proud of. I'm going to make every moment count.

✳

In the end, only three things matter: how much you loved, how gently you lived, and how gracefully you let go of things not meant for you. — ANONYMOUS

I Love You

Pablo Picasso once said, "Only put off until tomorrow what you are willing to die having left undone." I could put a lot of things in the pile of nonessentials: cleaning my garage, washing my car, stepping on the bathroom scale, trying exotic foods like alligator-tail tacos or turtle soup. But there's a big ol' pile of things that I would regret—very much—if I left them undone. And letting my loved ones know that I love them is on the top of the heap.

I know they already know it. I know they all know they're loved beyond reason. I know that. I do. But what if today is such a rough day that they don't? So, I will say *I love you* every chance I get. If I can't say *I love you* with words, I will say it with actions. And if I can't do that, I'll find a way to fling an *I love you* over the miles in some unorthodox manner; it doesn't matter how the message gets there . . . it just has to get there.

There's always tomorrow. Except when there isn't.

I love you, I love you, I love you.

Never pass up an opportunity to tell your loved ones you love them. — SHARON WALTERS

Fierce

My hands may be tied, but that doesn't mean I can't unleash the protective fury that addiction has wrought. I may hate The Addict, but I love my child, and everything I do can still reflect that. I may be hobbled, but I am *fierce*.

I will channel my need to do something for my child into something that *means* something. For *him*. Even if he's nowhere around. I will put my energies into doing something with real heft and might.

I will use my power wisely: I will *not* do something just for the sake of doing something. I will *not* do something just because it makes *me* feel good, when it actually might hurt the son that I love. I will *not* do something for him when doing nothing might be the better way to go.

Instead, I will speak out about addiction. This is something I can do for my son without hurting him. My direct influence on him may be restricted, but I'm not completely bound and gagged. For my son, I will educate anyone who will listen. I will defend the truth. I will open eyes and hearts and minds.

This year I will be stronger, braver, kinder, and unstoppable. This year I will be fierce. — ANONYMOUS

With the Heart of Another

I know what it's like to feel all alone in roomful of people. I know what it's like to feel like I haven't been heard. I know what it's like to be loved by people who have no idea of the feelings I feel.

I truly understand how most people can't grasp what it means to be the mom of an addict (and all that entails)—I can hardly grasp it, and I'm living it. But my situation isn't the only one that's not being grasped. People all around me are carrying the burden of traumas I've only fleetingly imagined: lost jobs, teen pregnancies, sexual abuse. Parents who are dying, sons who are off fighting a war. Grandparents with dementia. Kids who've lost a leg. Unimaginable stories with dark details that have gone unseen by me.

Now, I will look outside of myself. I will make the effort of trying to understand the different roads that people are on. So different, yet the same? And I will try to help them to feel less alone. I will slip myself into the eyes and ears and hearts of the people around me, like slipping myself into their shoes. Feeling their pinched toes. And wearing their salty tears.

*

Seeing with the eyes of another, listening with the ears of another, and feeling with the heart of another.

— ALFRED ADLER

A Bounty of Beauty

The sunrise, the sunset. A sunflower. A carpet of tulips. Fluffy clouds, autumn leaves, snowcapped mountains, and raindrops. Playful puppies, a bird's song. The fluttering of butterflies. A symphony. A waltz. The smile of a stranger, and children who are laughing. A pair of shiny black high-heeled shoes. Falling stars. And hugs.

A bounty of beauty is around me. But I will create even more. And I'll reap the benefits of the happy harvest I did sow, filling my soul by filling my eyes.

I will plant a garden full of purples and yellows and happy, happy daisies. I will paint a picture using brightly colored paints. I will decorate cupcakes with oodles of frosting, and I'll cook up a gorgeous roast beef. I will set a dinner table with napkins folded into swans. I will put on a pretty outfit. I will polish my toes in pink. An abundance. A plethora. A profusion of artistic adornment.

Beauty. Who can get too much of that?

∗

Whenever you are creating beauty around you, you are restoring your own soul. — ALICE WALKER

The Purpose of Purpose

It's easy to forget, in the hubbub of life, that my purpose here is to make—and leave—the world a better place. No matter what happens around me.

My purpose doesn't have to be grand or showy. It can be simple. And quiet. And shuffle along like a tortoise, one slow-and-steady day at a time. I can take my unique talents, whatever they may be, and use them to touch one person at a time or to touch a whole crowd of people. No matter how I proceed, I will make an impact. My hands and feet and motherly arms have a purpose to fulfill that is bigger than me. I don't need any credit; no one even has to know what I do.

We are born. We die. In between those two momentous occasions we have the potential to make and leave the world a better place: the purpose of purpose.

One day, one choice.

I vow that my time here on earth will not be wasted.

The meaning of life is to find your gift. The purpose of life is to give it away. — DAVID VISCOTT

The Power of One

Today I will tell one person that I love an addict. Tomorrow I will tell one more. And the day after that, yet another. I've got a message to spread; I will sprinkle my words around like a handful of seeds.

There is no shame in addiction. Ironically, it's shame that holds most people back. But by talking openly, *casually*, about addiction, the shame and stigma surrounding it will eventually disappear.

I don't need to share all the gory details when slipping my public service announcement off-handedly into chats. And I don't need to project an image of *poor me*. I simply want to make people aware that addiction is happening right in their midst—not always hidden in some dark, grungy corner.

Addiction is a disease; just like any other disease, it can happen to anyone, and it's not something to be ashamed of. The more this message is put into words, the more it will be absorbed and understood. My goal is that the conventional wisdom surrounding addiction will finally, actually, be *correct* wisdom.

One seed can start a garden, one candle can light a room, one voice can start the conversation.

One day, one word, one step at a time.

✳

If you think you're too small to make a difference, try sleeping with a mosquito in the room. — DALAI LAMA XIV

Branches of the Same Tree

I don't have all the answers. To be honest, I have very few. The truth is, *nobody* has all the answers—*everybody* is still trying to figure addiction out. But each of us has a unique experience, a unique perspective, to share. We're all branches of the same tree—and the root is addiction.

We all have our own angle. Our own strengths. Our own arena in which we shine. Our own particular area of focus is influenced by the particular form of devastation inflicted upon our own particular life.

We can bring awareness to and about addiction, addicts, and the people who love them in a number of ways. Some people write books or articles, publish magazines, or host radio shows. Some start grassroots organizations or organize candlelight vigils, fundraisers, and 5K runs. Some get the word out about medication-assisted interventions and treatments; others get involved with the judicial system and laws. Each particular aspect of addiction is getting covered, somewhere, by someone, in a uniquely important way. And, *together,* our snapshots create a panoramic scene: together, we create a comprehensive picture of addiction for the world to see.

✳

A bird does not sing because he has an answer. He sings because he has a song. — JOAN WALSH ANGLUND

A Hug between Souls

It's impossible to tell, just by looking, what burdens the people I meet are carrying around. People are adept at minding their millstones.

It's impossible to tell, just by looking, if the grocery store clerk is feeling such utter despair that she's barely able to refrain from crying. It's impossible to tell what sadness the server at lunch has hidden away beneath her carefully painted-on mask and pink lipstick. It's impossible to tell what pain the florist swallowed down this morning with her breakfast. Yes, it may be impossible to tell what burdens the people I meet are carrying around, but I happen to have a magic elixir for their sadness.

A smile. *A smile is a hug between souls.*

I know what it's like to pretend a happy way through a very unhappy day. I know what it's like to fake joy when I've lost hope. And I know what it's like when someone, anyone, shoots me a smile, especially when I'm feeling down.

So, I will pass out my hug-filled smiles freely.

❋

Some people make your laugh a little louder, your smile a little brighter, and your life a little better. Try to be one of those people. — ANONYMOUS

Scoff Not

Twenty people could stand on a beach, watching the same sunrise, and, if asked, describe what unfolded before them with delightfully different details. What each person sees is influenced by innumerable factors, happening right up to the moment the sun peeked up from the horizon. So it is with life. We each come to our own understanding of what life puts before us in our own time, influenced by experiences as unique as our fingerprints.

Differences in perception—all differences—make the world an interesting and vibrant place. So, too, do differences of opinion. I will listen with respect, suspending my own preconceived notions as I try to comprehend and understand differing positions. I do not always have to be right, and I can agreeably agree to disagree if there's something with which I don't see eye-to-eye.

I don't want to engage in the ugliness of scoffing and scorning, judging and jeering; this is all self-righteous and smug. And I don't want the thoughts and beliefs that make me *me* to be the ones that are ridiculed next.

Scoff not—not even inside my own head.

✳

Just because you don't understand something doesn't mean it's nonsense. — LEMONY SNICKET

Afloat

The individual stories of the people who love the *twenty-three million addicts* in our country hold immeasurable moments of suffering and loneliness, crying and praying. It's imponderable, really, the excruciating details of the day-to-day dramas and traumas, fears, worries, and struggles. The goings-on behind the scenes, behind closed doors, and behind carefully groomed masks.

It's all just too vast, too deep. It's as devastating and incomprehensible as a thousand-year flood. Beaten, bewildered, hopeless, and trying to cope, we still need to reach out and help to keep each other afloat.

It's imponderable, really, the pain and hard work extracted from me in trying to survive my child's addiction. Just as imponderable would be not trying to turn that pain and hard work into something meaningful. Something that *means* something. Something that lasts. So, I will reach out to help others from sinking, even though I'm still struggling to survive. I will hoist them into my life raft. We can cling to it together, hanging on for dear life.

*

Your greatest display of strength and character in life comes at the time when you are able to help someone else while going through your own storm. — ANONYMOUS

Hugs and Hope

Hug the mom of an addict today; addiction makes people so uncomfortable, she's often left to suffer in great pain all alone. Hug the dad of an addict today; addiction is so misunderstood, he's made to carry a steaming pile of shame. Hug the brother or sister of an addict today; addiction is so consuming, they've not only been lost in the shuffle, they've also lost life's very first friend. Hug the grandparents of an addict today; addiction changes grandchildren so completely, they're confused about what to do or not do.

Hug the police, paramedics, doctors, and nurses today; addiction tries so hard to kill our children, and these angels are on the front line trying to save them. Hug the friend and the acquaintance, the counselor and the interventionist today; addiction is so complicated, it takes a whole village to make it through. Hug the person who didn't enable your child today; addiction is so conniving, it's very hard to not be tricked into letting the addict do the thing he wants to do.

Hug an addict today (even if he's not your own); addiction isn't something he wanted—remember that he's living a very tortured life.

Near and far. Sending hugs—and hope—to you all.

When my arms cannot reach people who are close to my heart, I always hug them with my prayers. — ANONYMOUS

I've Got Joy Down in My Heart

Before children, my heart had never known such joy. Because of them, I've known the magic of holding chubby little hands, hearing little voices say *I wuv you, Mommy,* and of vicariously discovering toes and caterpillars and girls. My heart has burst with the joy of it all.

It has also imploded with great pain.

But that's what happens with great love. The good and the bad. The ice and the fire. The whole wacky gamut comes with the job of being a mother. And I wouldn't trade it for anything.

There's agony in allowing happiness into my life again, after addiction put a noose on my child, but there's also peace to be found: I'm honoring my son by putting joy in the place where he should be.

I've got joy, joy, joy, joy down in my heart,
Down in my heart, down in my heart,
I've got joy, joy, joy, joy down in my heart,
Down in my heart to stay.

— GEORGE WILLIS COOKE

Love Story

If a mother's love could fix addiction, it would have long ago been eradicated—too many people don't understand this. So, I will tell my story. *My love story.* With my words, I will open a door and let in some light.

Come along. Take my hand. Here, let's put on our shoes and take a walk. We'll be stepping into an uncomfortable world you've not yet explored, but we'll take it slow, with baby steps. See. And feel. And cry. You might be exhausted after walking beside me, through my life.

If a mother's love could fix addiction, it would have long ago been eradicated—too many mothers of addicts struggle to understand this. So, I will tell my story. *My love story.* With my words, I will open a door and let in some light.

Come along. Take my hand. Let's walk this sad and scary path together. We'll be stepping into a gloomy world we know all too well, but we'll take it slow, with baby steps. See. And feel. And cry. You might find comfort and healing in knowing you're not traveling alone.

✳

Your story will heal you and your story will heal somebody else. When you tell your story, you free yourself and give other people permission to acknowledge their own story.

— IYANLA VANZANT

Uplifted

We are a sisterhood. A club. A flock. We are moms who love a child suffering with the disease of addiction, and together we are a mighty force. I never would have wanted to be a part of this group, but now that I am, I'm immensely grateful for the love and support. Bonded in spirit, we are carried forward, onward, and upward on the wings of one another's strengths.

Bonded by heartache and a tormented maternal love, we've known each other forever—even if we've never met. Don't ruffle our feathers—our defensive instincts are strong; together we take care of all the other moms. We validate. We protect. We take the frightened and the fallen under our wings, keeping them safe until they are able to brave the storm. We understand feelings of utter failure (even though failures we are not). We are the moms of addicts. And we are not alone.

There is strength and power in numbers. Uplifted by one another, we're like a gaggle of amazing geese.

Like the geese, people who share a common direction and a sense of community can get where they're going quicker and easier because they are traveling on the thrust of one another. — ANONYMOUS

Slow and Steady

Patience is a virtue. Like a river, it flows—slow and steady—for a long, long time. Patience is the act of waiting. And so, a lot of the time, patience is a strain on my patience. Patience is the art of *hope* and *inner peace,* one that I'm patiently waiting to perfect. Patience is tolerating delays and enduring an unhurried pace. Patience is the act of stepping back, staying put, until the time is right. Patience is waiting around while keeping a good attitude. *Sigh.*

Patience is enjoying the moment for the moment. Patience is subtle, not white-knuckled or coiled up like a spring. Patience is a gift to myself and to others; breathing down necks with annoyance just makes everyone upset. Patience is determination and peace and compassion all rolled up into one. Patience is giving somebody else the time they deserve and not shoving my time frame down their throat.

Patience is counting down before blasting off.

Patience is not the ability to wait, but how you act while you're waiting. — JOYCE MEYER

Seeds of Kindness

I believe we all have a purpose here on earth. Something we need to do before we go on to the next great place. I believe we are here to fill with love the lives of those we touch. I believe that love starts at home; we provide our family with time and love, patience and understanding, and then we move out from there with more time and love, patience and understanding.

And so do they.

And then it spreads.

For every pain I have ever felt, I will try to erase one. For every hateful word, I will sow a handful of love.

I will fill the lives of those I touch with respect and honesty, loyalty and kindness. And so will they. And so, respect and honesty, loyalty and kindness will spread, like a scattering of seeds. Drifting, blowing. Breezing into the lives of those I cannot reach on my own.

*

In scattering seeds of kindness, do it by hand and not by machine. — GEORGE ADE

One Kind Thing

Kindness is contagious. Once it gets going, it keeps getting passed around. So, I'm going to do one kind thing every day. (Bonus points if I reach out to a stranger or keep the thing I do a secret.) Big or small. From the heart. Whatever moves me to move.

There are so many possibilities: I can open a door. I can tip big. I can give a compliment, a warm meal, or a ride. I can stop at crosswalks (rather than breezing through, pretending I didn't see). I can let someone into the grocery line, car lane, or parking spot rather than barging ahead. I can share my umbrella in a sudden downpour. I can put a quarter in a meter that's running out of time. I can write letters to the troops, volunteer at a soup kitchen, or teach someone to read.

I can refrain myself from gossip, from interrupting. This is an act of kindness, too. I can set my phone aside. I can listen. Smile. Be patient. Tell the truth. I can say thank you. I can dole out big hugs.

I can call my mom.

*

Ah, kindness. What a simple way to tell another struggling soul that there is love to be found in this world. —A. A. MALEE

Together We Are Stronger

When I first was struggling to understand my child's addiction and this horrible place where love and addiction meet, there weren't as many resources or outspoken voices as there are today. We've come a long way in recognizing that families—parents, grandparents, spouses, children, and siblings—are all faces and voices and victims of addiction, too. In addition to the old faithfuls, Al-Anon and Families Anonymous, organizations such as *Family Recovery Network, Moms Can, The Addict's Mom, Families of Addicts, Changing Lives Foundation, Magnolia New Beginnings, Attack Addiction,* and *Parent Pathway* have sprung from the deep well of need and can help us to keep (or find) our sanity and get some perspective. They are there to help us. And to help us feel less alone. Together we are stronger.

Like the wind singing through a forest of sturdy branches, let us be one strong voice against addiction.

One voice is a mere whisper. A chorus of voices can change the world. — GARY MENDELL

List of Meditations

Part One: Take Root, 3

Part Two: grow, Grow, GROW, 43

Part Three: Wilt (a Bit), 101

Part Five: Bloom, 161

Part Six: Scatter Goodness, 215

Acknowledgments

I would like to thank Hazelden Publishing—the whole team—for working so hard to make *Tending Dandelions* such a beautiful book; I am truly honored. I would especially like to thank Vanessa Torrado—more than an encouraging editor, she has been a soul sister from day one. And Heather Silsbee, who has so smoothly helped carry things through to the end.

I would like to thank Cynthia Khan, Yvette Stowers, and Laurie Ward—three sweet friends and first readers.

And, mostly, I would like to thank my children, who live in my heart and on every page.

About the Author

Sandra Swenson is the mother of two sons—one of whom struggles with addiction. A voice for the loved ones of addicts, she first documented her experiences with her son's addiction in the critically acclaimed book *The Joey Song: A Mother's Story of Her Son's Addiction*. An advocate for acceptance, education, healing, and recovery, Sandra lives near Austin, Texas.

When she's not working in her garden, reading, traveling, or volunteering, she can be found sharing her journey through the place where love and addiction meet.

You can connect with her on social media as well as through her website, SandySwenson.com.

About Hazelden Publishing

As part of the Hazelden Betty Ford Foundation, Hazelden Publishing offers both cutting-edge educational resources and inspirational books. Our print and digital works help guide individuals in treatment and recovery, and their loved ones. Professionals who work to prevent and treat addiction also turn to Hazelden Publishing for evidence-based curricula, digital content solutions, and videos for use in schools, treatment programs, correctional programs, and electronic health records systems. We also offer training for implementation of our curricula.

Through published and digital works, Hazelden Publishing extends the reach of healing and hope to individuals, families, and communities affected by addiction and related issues.

For more information about Hazelden publications, please call **800-328-9000** or visit us online at **hazelden.org/bookstore.**

Other Titles That May Interest You

Addict in the Family
Stories of Loss, Hope, and Recovery
BEVERLY CONYERS

Gripping stories of fathers, mothers, sons, and daughters of addicts offer important lessons on loving, detachment, intervention, and self-care.

Order No. 1018, also available as an e-book

Today's Gift
Daily Meditations for Families

The tensions and joys that can help a family care for all its members are explored in these 366 meditations that nurture family esteem and strengthen family bonds.

Order No. 1031, also available as an e-book

The Promise of a New Day
A Book of Daily Meditations
KAREN CASEY AND MARTHA VANCEBURG

The Promise of a New Day offers daily reflections for simple, inspiring wisdom about creating and maintaining inner peace.

Order No. 1045, also available as an e-book

For more information or to order these or other resources from Hazelden Publishing,
call **800-328-9000** or visit **hazelden.org/bookstore**.